My Family and
Other Animals

LEVEL THREE   1000 HEADWORDS

OXFORD
UNIVERSITY PRESS

Great Clarendon Street, Oxford OX2 6DP

Oxford University Press is a department of the University of Oxford. It furthers the University's objective of excellence in research, scholarship, and education by publishing worldwide in

Oxford New York

Auckland Cape Town Dar es Salaam Hong Kong Karachi Kuala Lumpur Madrid Melbourne Mexico City Nairobi New Delhi Shanghai Taipei Toronto

With offices in

Argentina Austria Brazil Chile Czech Republic France Greece Guatemala Hungary Italy Japan Poland Portugal Singapore South Korea Switzerland Thailand Turkey Ukraine Vietnam

OXFORD and OXFORD ENGLISH are registered trade marks of Oxford University Press in the UK and in certain other countries

This edition © Oxford University Press 2010

The moral rights of the author have been asserted

Database right Oxford University Press (maker)

First published in Dominoes 2003

2014 2013 2012 2011 2010

10 9 8 7 6 5 4 3 2 1

ISBN: 978 0 19 424824 2 BOOK
ISBN: 978 0 19 424782 5 BOOK AND MULTIROM PACK
MULTIROM NOT AVAILABLE SEPARATELY

Any websites referred to in this publication are in the public domain and their addresses are provided by Oxford University Press for information only. Oxford University Press disclaims any responsibility for the content

Printed in China

ACKNOWLEDGEMENTS

The publisher would like to thank the following for permission to reproduce photographs: Art Directors and Trip Photo Library pp iv (Olive tree/B Turner), iv (Cypress trees/B Turner), 1 (Corfu coast/B Turner), 6 (Glass jam jar/Helene Rogers), 6 (Stuffed olives), 54 (Corfu/B Turner), 63 (Corfu/Bob Turner); Christopher Sheehan pp11, 21, 57, 69, 77; Cody Images p44 (Seaplane, Macchi Aviation Company/TRH Pictures); Corbis pp 70 (Herring gull/Ann Sheffield Jacobi), 70 (Circus tent/Bruce Adams/Eye Ubiquitous), 70 (Natural chloride mining area/Paul Edmondson), 70 (Bird market in China/Derek M. Allan; Travel Ink); FLPA pp27 & 75 (Scorpion/Silvestris), 41 (Scorpion carrying young/ Silvestris Fotoservice), 58 (Praying mantis/Hans Dieter Brandl), 64 & 70 (Terrapin/Roger Tidman), 66 (Gull/Martin B Withers); Gerald Durrell Collection pp2, 14, 23, 28, 32, 37, 39, 45, 49, 51, 52, 78, 80, 81, 83; Getty Images pp3 (Corfu harbour, 1930/Hulton Archive), 7 (London street/ Hulton Archive), 9 (Greek Islands, Corfu Piazza Della Pigna/Popperfoto), 30 (Corfu Harbour/Hulton Archive); 82 (Greek Islands, Corfu Piazza Della Pigna/Popperfoto); Nature Picture Library pp53 & 79 (Harbour porpoise/ Florian Graner); NHPA pp iv & 19 (Yellow scorpion/Daniel Heuclin), 20 (Hermann's tortoise/Daniel Heuclin), 61 (Common toad/Manfred Danegger), 65 (Grass snake in water/Mike Lane); OUP pp iv (Grapes/Corel), 6 (Nautilus/ Photodisc), 7 (Caterpillar/Photodisc), 12 (Black grapes/ Ingram), 15 & 47 (Beetles/Ingram), 19 (Spider/Photodisc), 24 (Pigeon/Photodisc), 31 (Wing detail/Digital Vision), 70 (Game of chess/Ingram), 71 (Sunset by the sea); Photolibrary pp iv & 19 (Donkeys/Ronald Toms), 15 & 47 (Ladybird spider/Manfred Pfefferie/OSF), 19 (Stag beetle/ Berndt Fischer/OSF), 19 (Wood pigeon/Mark Hamblin), 29 & 62 (Trapdoor spider), 74 (Cicada/Paolo de Oliveira), 76 (Praying mantis/Manfred Pfefferie/OSF); Photoshot pp iv & 19 (Green lizard/Hans Reinhard), iv (Figs), 6 (Butterfly/Kim Taylor), 15 & 19(Ladybird/Andrew Purcell), 17 (Green lizard/P Kaya), 19 (Tortoise/Werner Layer), 40 & 76 (Gecko/P Kaya); Pictures Colour Library Ltd pp iv & 19 (Goat/Terry Harris), 5 (Ionian, Corfu Town/Terry Harris); Travel-Ink pp7 (Horse & carriage/Simon Reddy), 19 (Cottage/Jeff Hammond).

Cover: Corbis pp (young boy watches tortoise/Ty Milford/ Aurora Open)

DOMINOES

Series Editors: Bill Bowler and Sue Parminter

My Family and Other Animals

Gerald Durrell

Text adaptation by Bill Bowler

Gerald Durrell was born in India in 1925. His father died when he was only three and soon after that his family returned to England. In 1935 they went to live on the island of Corfu. It was here that Gerald's great interest in natural history grew, and where he kept many wild animals as pets. Gerald got his first job back in England as a zookeeper at Whipsnade Zoo, north of London. Later, he travelled all over the world to study and film animals. He soon realized that many animals were in danger and needed saving. In 1958 he opened his own zoo in Jersey. Gerald Durrell wrote many books – most of them about his work with animals. He died in 1995.

OXFORD

UNIVERSITY PRESS

BEFORE READING

1 **You can find all these things
on Mediterranean islands.
Match the words with the
pictures. Use a dictionary
to help you.**

a ☐ cypress trees
b ☐ donkeys
c ☐ figs
d ☐ goat
e ☐ grapes
f ☐ lizard
g ☐ olive tree
h ☐ scorpion

2 **You are going to an island in the Mediterranean. What would you like to do there?
Tick four boxes.**

a ☐ swim in the sea
b ☐ find and catch island animals
c ☐ meet and talk to people on the island
d ☐ take photos

e ☐ sail round the island
f ☐ write a diary
g ☐ lie on the beach
h ☐ eat sea food

3 **Talk about your ideas with a partner.**

CHAPTER 1

How it all began

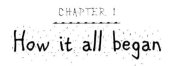

This is the story of the five years when my family and I stayed on the Greek island of Corfu. At first I wanted to write about the **natural history** of the island, but I made the mistake of introducing my family into the book in the first few pages. Once they were on paper they made themselves at home and invited their friends to join them. It was only with great difficulty that I managed to **concentrate** on animals here and there.

   I have tried to give a true picture of my family in these pages. At the start of my story Larry, the oldest, was twenty-three, Leslie was nineteen, Margo was eighteen, and I, at ten years old, was the youngest. We have never really known how old Mother is because she can never remember the year that she was born. My mother also asks me to explain that our father had died some years before the story begins, for, as she rightly says, you never know what people will think.

It all began in the summer of 1935. July was finished and, as often happens in England, August brought with it a cold wind

natural history
the study of plants
and animals

concentrate to
study or think
carefully about
only one thing

*The island
of Corfu*

1

*Gerald (aged 8)
with his mother*

and a heavy sky. It was raining on Bournemouth beach and the sea was angry-looking. It was just the kind of weather to make anyone feel awful.

That afternoon all my family were ill. I was lying on the floor looking at the **shells** that I had found on the beach. I had a heavy cold, which meant that I had to **breathe** through my mouth instead of my nose. My brother Leslie was sitting by the fire. His ears were aching terribly. My sister Margo had red **spots** all over her face. The cold weather made my mother's fingers ache. Only my brother Larry was in good health, but he felt terrible for all of us.

It was Larry, of course, who started it.

'Why do we stay in this awful country?' he asked, looking out of the window at the rain. 'Look at us! We're just like pictures out of a doctor's book of illnesses. And you Mother, you're looking older every day.'

Mother stared at him over the top of her book *Indian Cooking for Beginners*.

'I am not!' she said, and then went back to her reading.

'You are!' Larry went on. 'What we need is lots of lovely sun and a country where we can grow. Don't you agree, Les?'

Leslie put a hand to one ear. 'What did you say?' he asked.

'There, you see. I can't hold a conversation with either of my brothers. Les can't hear and Gerry,' said Larry looking at me, 'can't speak clearly. We must do something. I really can't concentrate on writing in a house full of sick people.'

'Yes, dear,' said Mother, not really listening to him.

'I had a letter from my friend George this morning. He says that Corfu's wonderful. Why don't we sell this house, pack our bags, and go to Corfu?'

'Oh, no, dear,' said Mother, putting down her Indian food

shell the hard outside part of a small animal

breathe to make air move into and out of your body through your nose and mouth

spot a small round thing on the skin that has a different colour; young people often get spots

book at last and turning to Larry. 'We can't possibly sell this house. I've only just bought it.'

But in the end we sold the house and left the awfulness of the English summer, like birds that fly south to warmer parts.

Each of us took with us what we thought was important. Margo's bags were full of pretty summer clothes, books on eating healthily, and lots of bottles of medicine for spots. Leslie took two shirts and two pairs of trousers, three guns and a book on taking care of them. Larry took two big boxes of books and a very small bag of clothes. Mother sensibly took clothes in one bag and books on cooking and gardens in another bag. I took with me some natural history books, a **net** for catching **butterflies**, my dog Roger, and a **jar** full of fat, sleepy **caterpillars**.

And so we left wet, cold England and passed through rainy, sad France, snowy Switzerland, and noisy, happy, smelly Italy. At last one evening we left the south of Italy on a little ship and sailed across the sea to Corfu. Early the next day we left our beds and went to look across the purple water at the magic island that was getting closer every minute. Soon we could see the brown mountains, the green of the **olive** trees, the white beaches and the gold, red and white rocks at the sea's edge. And when we were very close, we could hear the high ringing voices of the **cicadas** above the noise of the ship's engine.

net an open bag with small holes in it that you can use for catching fish or other things

butterfly (*plural* **butterflies**) a small animal like a fly with big brightly-coloured wings

jar a glass container for food, for example, a coffee jar

caterpillar a small long animal with a lot of legs; it becomes a butterfly

olive a small green or black fruit, with a salty taste

cicada a large insect with colourless wings that lives in hot countries and makes a loud, high noise by moving its back legs against each other

Corfu harbour, 1930

3

When we landed, Larry left the ship first, keeping a careful eye on the men who were carrying his heavy boxes off the ship. Leslie followed him, short and sporty, with the strong look of a fighter in his eye. Then came Margo, smelling very sweet in a flowery dress. Mother came next, but she was immediately pulled by Roger over to the nearest **lamp post**.

Larry went off and found two wonderful old **cabs** pulled by horses to take us to our hotel. One was for us and the other was for our bags. He sat down in the first cab and then looked round.

'Well?' he asked. 'What are we waiting for?'

'Mother,' explained Leslie. 'Roger's found a lamp post.'

'Oh no!' said Larry, and he shouted, 'Come on, Mother. Can't the dog wait?'

'Coming dear!' called Mother.

'That dog has been a problem all the way,' said Larry.

At that moment Mother arrived with Roger and tried to make him climb into the cab. Now Roger had never been in a cab pulled by horses before, and he didn't want to get in at all. In the end we had to pick him up, throw him in, jump in after him and sit on him to stop him from getting out again. But then the horse got frightened and began to move off and we all fell about in the bottom of the cab with Roger **barking** unhappily under us.

Larry was not amused.

'I had wanted us to arrive like kings and this is what happens . . . we look just like a group of travelling actors.'

'Don't worry, dear,' said Mother calmly. 'We'll soon be at the hotel.'

lamp post a tall post in the street with a light at the top

cab taxi

bark (of a dog) to make a short loud noise

When we arrived at the hotel, we saw that lots of street dogs had come out of nowhere to bark at this strange lazy black English dog that travelled in a cab. We didn't want a dog fight to start, so Larry jumped down and danced through the barking dogs, clearing the way for us to follow by waving a magazine about in front of him. And after him Leslie, Margo, Mother, and I carried Roger, barking and biting, into the hotel, closing the door quickly behind us.

The hotel manager came towards us with a worried look on his face.

Mother's hat was on one side of her head and she was holding my jar of caterpillars in her hand. But she spoke to the manager calmly, and pretended that there was nothing unusual in the way that we had entered his hotel.

'Our name's Durrell,' she said. 'I believe that you have some rooms for us.'

'Yes, madam,' said the manager, walking carefully past the still barking Roger to get the keys. 'Four rooms on the first floor.'

'How nice,' smiled Mother. 'Then I think we'll go straight up and have a little rest before lunch.'

And, like a queen, she took her family upstairs.

Corfu town today

READING CHECK

Choose the right words to finish the sentences.

a Larry wants to go to Corfu because . . .
  1 ☑ the weather is better there.
  2 ☐ he has a bad cold.
  3 ☐ he doesn't like English cooking.

b At first Mother . . .
  1 ☐ thinks going to Corfu is a great idea.
  2 ☐ doesn't want to sell the house that she's just bought.
  3 ☐ wants to learn more about Indian cooking.

c To take to Corfu, Leslie packs . . .
  1 ☐ books on cooking and gardening.
  2 ☐ summer clothes and medicine.
  3 ☐ some clothes and some guns.

d When they arrive in Corfu, Mother . . .
  1 ☐ buys some sweets and some flowers.
  2 ☐ looks for a cab.
  3 ☐ waits for a while by a lamp post with Roger.

e When they arrive at the hotel, Larry tries to . . .
  1 ☐ go dancing.
  2 ☐ read a magazine.
  3 ☐ stop a dog fight.

f The hotel manager . . .
  1 ☐ is worried about the Durrell family staying at the hotel.
  2 ☐ thinks the Durrells are kings and queens.
  3 ☐ welcomes the Durrell family happily.

WORD WORK

1 Match the words with the correct pictures.

a ~~lamp post~~
  butterfly...

b caterpillar
  . . . .

c olives
  . . . .

d butterfly
  . . . .

e shell

....

g jar

....

f cab

....

2 Find words in the ships to complete the sentences.

a At the start of the story Gerry has a cold
and can't ..breathe.... very well.

t e r a h b e

b Larry can't really...................... on his writing when
he has lots of sick people all around him.

t o n t c e r a c e n

c Roger .... when
the Durrells go into the hotel.

s a k r b

d Because Margo wants to look beautiful, she doesn't
like having lots of .... on her face.

t o s p s

e You can often hear ....
in the trees in hot countries.

i d s a c c a

f Gerry is most interested in studying ....
.... more than anything.

l a r a n u t   t i r y s h o

GUESS WHAT

What do you think happens in the next chapter? Tick two boxes.

a ☐ Mother doesn't like the food at the hotel.

b ☐ The hotel manager asks the Durrells to leave because they are too noisy.

c ☐ Larry's friend George helps the Durrells to find a house.

d ☐ Mother has problems finding a house with a bathroom.

e ☐ The Durrells make friends with a Greek person who can speak English.

CHAPTER 2

A villa with a bathroom

Unluckily our hotel was opposite the **cemetery**. As we sat in our rooms, looking out of the windows, we saw lots of **funerals** go by. For each funeral six or seven black cabs, pulled by black horses, and full of crying family and friends dressed in black, made their way into the cemetery. Then came the **coffin** on a **cart**, also pulled by horses. Some coffins were white, others were black. They all looked like big birthday cakes covered in a sea of flowers. The people of Corfu clearly thought that the best part of dying was the funeral and when I saw their funerals, I had to agree. Mother did not see it the same way.

'I'm sure it's an **epidemic**!' she said. 'So many of them all at once. It's not natural.'

'Mother. There's nothing unnatural about dying. People do it all the time!' said Larry.

'Yes, but so many of them at the same time. I'm sure something's wrong.'

'Perhaps they save them up and **bury** them together,' said Leslie unfeelingly.

'No, I'm sure it's the toilets here. Haven't you noticed the smell? And there's no paper in them! Most unhealthy!'

Margo's face went green. 'I think I feel ill! Perhaps I'm getting it, too.'

'Don't be **silly** dear. Maybe it isn't the kind of illness you can catch easily!'

'But an epidemic is always an illness that people catch easily!' said Leslie sensibly.

'Well,' said Mother, 'then we'll have to move. We must find a house in the country at once.'

The next morning we went looking for houses. Mr Beeler,

cemetery a place where dead people are put under the ground

funeral the time when a dead person is put under the ground

coffin a box that you put a dead person's body in

cart an open wooden car that horses pull

epidemic when a lot of people have the same illness at the same time

bury to put a dead body under the ground

silly stupid

a fat little man who worked at the hotel, went with us. He looked full of life when we started out, but after showing us a number of **villas** in different places on the island, he began to look very tired.

'Mrs Durrell,' he said. 'I have shown you every villa that I know and you do not want any of them. What is the matter?'

Mother looked at him in surprise.

'But didn't you notice? None of them had a bathroom.'

Mr Beeler's eyes grew big and round.

'Mrs Durrell,' he said. 'Why do you need a bathroom? Haven't you got the sea?'

We went back to the hotel in silence.

The next day Mother decided that we should take a taxi and go looking for houses by ourselves. She still wanted a villa with a bathroom.

When we got to the big square in the centre of the town the taxi drivers all got out of their cars, stood round us and began shouting at us. To us it seemed like an argument, but in fact each man was only trying to get us to choose his taxi.

'Do something!' said Mother helplessly. 'Tell them that we don't understand them.'

villa a house in the country with a large garden, especially in Southern Europe

Corfu town in the 1930s

9

Margo stepped forwards smiling.

'English! English!' she shouted. 'We don't understand Greek!'

At that moment a deep voice behind us called out.

'Hey! Why don't you choose someone who can speak your own language?'

We turned and saw an old Dodge car, with a short fat man at the wheel. He got out and came towards us. Then he stopped and stared at the other drivers angrily.

'Are they worrying you?' he asked.

'No, no,' lied Mother. 'We just couldn't understand them.'

'They are very bad men,' he said. 'They sell their own grandmothers for the right price. Excuse me!'

He turned and shouted at the other drivers in Greek and they went back to their cars. Then he turned back to us.

'Where do you want to go?' he asked.

'We are looking,' said Mother, 'for a villa with a bathroom.'

'Sure. I can take you,' he replied. 'Get into the car.'

We climbed into the car and he drove off fast, through the narrow streets of the town. We drove round carts, **donkeys** and dogs, and past groups of village women. And as we hurried on our driver spoke to us.

'You English? Thought so. English people always want bathrooms. I have a bathroom in my house. Spiro's my name. Spiro Hakiaopulos. I learnt my English in Chicago. Went to make money. Then after eight years I came back to Corfu with this car.'

We were now driving hurriedly along a dry white country road – past olive trees and fields of **vines** – and we suddenly stopped at the top of a hill.

'There you are,' said Spiro, looking down the valley. 'That's the villa with the bathroom, just like you wanted.'

Mother, who had kept her eyes shut during the drive, now opened them and looked. The sky was bright blue, the sea was shining, the olive trees were silvery-green and there was

donkey an animal like a small horse with long ears and a loud voice

vine a climbing plant; you can make wine from its fruit

The strawberry-pink villa today

a small **pink** villa halfway up the hill in the middle of the valley in front of her. It looked like a lovely pink **strawberry** lying on a green plate. The minute that we saw it, we knew that we wanted to live there.

So we moved into the strawberry-pink villa and we soon felt at home there in our different ways. Margo put on a **tiny** swimsuit and went to lie in the sun among the olive trees. In this way she made friends with a number of handsome young men from the nearby village, who came out of nowhere to help her when her chair needed moving, or when a fly was worrying her.

Larry unpacked his books and tried to write. But on the second morning he found it difficult to concentrate because someone from the village had tied a donkey to a tree outside his bedroom window. In the end Mother and I had to untie the donkey and take it away down the hill so that Larry could have some quiet.

Leslie had unpacked his guns, and from his bedroom window he was now trying to shoot an old tin off the garden wall. Larry got very angry at this because the loud bangs were once more stopping him from concentrating on his writing. So Mother made Leslie go and do his shooting some way from the house, which helped a little.

Mother too was feeling at home, busily cooking and looking after the garden. And Roger and I felt very happy, looking round the garden for hours.

pink a colour between red and white

strawberry a small, soft, red fruit

tiny very small

READING CHECK

Put these sentences in the correct order. Number them 1–9.

a ☐ Larry finds it difficult to write.

b ☐ The Durrells see lots of coffins going by outside their hotel.

c ☐ They meet Spiro and he helps them find somewhere to live.

d ☐ Mother makes Leslie do his shooting away from the house.

e ☐ The Durrells try to find a taxi in the square.

f ☐ They decide to look for somewhere to live in the country.

g ☐ They move into a pink villa with a bathroom.

h ☐ Mr Beeler takes the Durrells around the island to look at houses.

i ☐ Margo goes to lie in the sun in her swimsuit.

WORD WORK

1 Find words from Chapter 2 in the grapes.

2 Match the words in Activity 1 with the underlined words in these sentences.

a In Corfu some <u>boxes that you put dead people's bodies in</u> are black and some are white. ...coffins......

b People in Corfu seem to enjoy <u>the times when dead people are put under the ground</u>.
....

c The hotel where the Durrells are staying is opposite the <u>place where dead people are put under the ground</u>. ....

d People in Corfu like <u>putting under ground the dead bodies of</u> people with lots of flowers. ....

e Mother thinks there's a real <u>time when a lot of people have the same illness</u> on Corfu. ....

f Margo has a <u>very small</u> swimsuit. ....

g Mother wants a <u>house in the country</u> with a bathroom. ....

h Margo sometimes says <u>stupid</u> things. ....

i Spiro shows them a house which has <u>between red and white</u> walls. ....

j Sitting in a valley, the house with a bathroom looks like a <u>small, soft red fruit</u> on a green plate. ....

k People in Corfu sometimes travel by <u>open wooden cars that horses pull</u>. ....

l Gerry and Mother have to move a <u>small animal with long ears and a loud voice</u> from outside Larry's window. ....

3 **What are the extra letters in the grapes? Write them in order and find the name of the Durrell's hotel.**

P _ _ _ _ _ _   _ _ _ _ _ _

GUESS WHAT

What do you think happens in the next chapter? Tick the boxes.	Yes	No
a Gerry learns to speak Greek.	☐	☐
b Mother marries Spiro.	☐	☐
c Gerry finds interesting things to look at in the garden of the pink villa.	☐	☐
d Margo finds herself a handsome Greek boyfriend.	☐	☐
e Gerry goes to school in the village.	☐	☐
f Gerry makes friends with different people on the island.	☐	☐

CHAPTER 3

Insects and other friends

shocked very surprised at something bad

kiss to touch lovingly with your mouth

insect a very small animal with six legs

We were very happy in the strawberry-pink villa with Spiro taking care of us.

'Don't you worry, Mrs Durrell. Everybody here knows me. You won't have any problems,' he said.

He went shopping with us, told us how much to pay for things, and thought Mother was wonderful.

'Don't worry your mother,' he used to say.

'Why not?' asked Larry. 'She worries us.'

'Mr Larry! Don't say that!' said Spiro, **shocked**. 'You have a truly wonderful mother – you should get down every morning and **kiss** her feet!'

Spiro with Margo, Gerald and Mother

As for me, I spent hours in the garden, listening to the cries of the cicadas in the olive trees, and watching **insects**. I loved

looking at the green flies and the brightly-coloured **ladybirds** climbing up the **roses**. I enjoyed lying on my stomach watching the black **beetles** walking across the dry ground. I was also interested in the tiny little **spiders** that could change colour; put one on a red rose and it became as red as blood, put it on a white rose and the colour left it and it became as white as snow.

All these discoveries pleased me, and I always had to tell my family about them at once. I rushed into the house to tell everyone that the strange black caterpillars weren't really caterpillars, but young ladybirds; or that I had found out how some flies stuck their eggs to leaves; or that underneath an old tree branch I had discovered a funny little mother insect sitting on her tiny white eggs.

I also got to know the village girls who passed the garden every day on their donkeys. They laughed and talked loudly as they worked among the olive trees in their colourful clothes like bright and beautiful birds. In the mornings when they went to work they called hello to me, and in the evenings when they came home they gave me presents – yellow **grapes** still warm from the sun, or soft black **figs** with pink lines on them where their thin skin was broken.

As the days passed, I listened to the village people speaking and began to understand what they said. What had at first been a fast-moving sea of language, impossible to follow, now became sounds and words that started to mean something. Slowly and carefully I began to use some words myself. Our neighbours were very pleased with me for trying to learn their language. They listened patiently, concentrating carefully, while I got my tongue and teeth around the answer to a question that they had asked, and when I finished they always smiled at me.

In time I learnt their names, who was part of the same family, who was married to whom, and who wanted to marry

ladybird a small insect that is red or orange with dark spots

rose a plant with beautiful sweet-smelling white, red or yellow flowers

beetle an insect like a ladybird which is brown or black in colour

spider a small animal with eight legs that eats flies

grape a small green or purple fruit that we eat or make into wine; it grows on a vine

fig a small soft sweet fruit that grows on trees in hot countries

whom. I learnt where their **cottages** were, and when Roger and I walked past, the whole family usually jumped out, pleased to see us. They used to say hello, bring a chair for me to sit on, and give me some fruit to eat.

Every day on the island was special; time stood still, and we never wanted it to end. But then the following day would break out of the dark skin of night and be waiting untouched and new for us, like a shiny, colourful dream.

We ate breakfast in the garden under the orange trees. The sky was clear and bright and the flowers were half-asleep. Breakfast was usually eaten slowly and in silence for no one felt like talking so early in the morning, but by the end of the meal, after the coffee, bread and eggs, people began to explain their different plans for that day. I never spent any time on this, as my plans were always the same. Instead, I concentrated on eating my breakfast as quickly as possible.

'Must you eat so noisily?' Larry said in a voice full of pain.

'Eat more slowly, dear,' said Mother. 'There's no need to hurry!'

No need to hurry? With Roger waiting for me with his soft brown eyes? With the cicadas starting to make their music among the olive trees? With the island waiting, morning cool and as bright as a star, for me to visit it?

But I couldn't hope to explain these thoughts to my family, so I ate more slowly for a time until they stopped looking at me and then once more I began to push as much food into my mouth as I could.

Roger always went with me on my island visits in those days. And we made many friends. There was fat and happy old Agathi who lived in a little old cottage high up the hill. She was seventy years old, but full of life. She taught me lots of old island songs – happy farmers' songs, sad love songs, and funny songs too. We often sang them together sitting outside her front door.

cottage a small house in the country

Then there was Yani, a tall old man with a brown face and a big nose who kept **goats**.

I remember that Roger and I were digging a large green **lizard** out of its hole in a wall when we first met Yani. In fact we had decided that the job was hopeless and we were lying down for a rest under a **cypress** tree when we heard the goat bells ringing. Suddenly the goats were all round us, eating grass and plants hungrily. Then Yani was standing over me, his olive wood stick in his hand, his heavy boots by my head, his small black eyes looking down at me.

'Take care young English **lord**,' he said. 'If you go to sleep under a cypress tree you will wake up crazy.'

I don't know why, but for the people of the island my family and I were all lords and ladies.

'Does that happen with all trees?' I asked.

'No. Only cypresses,' he said. And then he walked off.

I got to know Yani very well, for I often met him as I walked round the island, and I sometimes went to visit him at his house where he gave me fruit and told me to be careful about one thing or another.

goat an animal like a sheep that has horns and lives on mountains; people keep goats for their milk and meat

lizard a small green animal with a long tail

cypress a tall, straight, dark-coloured tree

lord an important man

A green lizard

17

ACTIVITIES

READING CHECK

Correct nine more mistakes in the chapter summary.

wonderful

Spiro thinks that Mrs Durrell is ~~awful~~ and he tells Larry not to worry her. Gerry spends

hours in the house looking at flies and caterpillars and other things. The village girls

pass the garden of the pink villa on their bicycles every morning. They bring Gerry

presents of fruit in the evening on their way to work. The Durrells' Greek neighbours

like it when Gerry speaks in English to them. The Durrells eat breakfast in the kitchen

without speaking at first. After breakfast they talk about their plans for the day. Gerry

always eats his breakfast slowly and very quietly. Gerry visits his neighbours and learns

island dances from Agathi, a fat old woman who lives in a cottage on a hill. One day he

is lying under a tree in the country when a tall old man called Yani comes and speaks to

him. Yani tells Gerry that sleeping under that kind of tree makes people rich.

WORD WORK

1 Correct the boxed words in these sentences. They all come from Chapter 3.

  a There are **noses** in the garden of the pink villa. _roses_ ....

  b Yani is an old man who keeps **boats** . ...

  c Yani calls Gerry a young **cord** . ...

  d Spiro is **shopped** to hear Larry saying bad things about his mother.
    ....

  e Spiro says that Larry should **miss** his mother's feet every morning. ....

  f Gerry likes looking at **inserts** . ...

2 Use words from Chapter 3 to label the pictures.

a .cottage....   b ....   c ....   d ....

GUESS WHAT

In the next chapter Gerry starts looking after two animals. Which animals do you think they are? Tick two pictures.

a ☐ a tortoise   b ☐ a lizard   c ☐ a goat

d ☐ a pigeon   e ☐ a donkey   f ☐ a scorpion

CHAPTER 4

Pets and lessons

feather birds have these on their bodies to keep them warm and to help them fly

tortoise a slow-moving animal with a hard shell on its body

pet an animal that lives with you in your home

pigeon a fat white or grey bird that often lives in towns

Perhaps the most interesting person I met on my island walks was the Rose-beetle Man. He wore a green hat with **feathers** stuck in it and a number of golden-green rose-beetles tied to it, and he had an old coat with pockets full of things to sell.

When we first met I soon realized that he couldn't speak, but by moving his hands, his arms, his face, his mouth and eyes, he could get his message across.

That first time we met, I bought a **tortoise** from him. I called him Achilles, and he was an intelligent and loving **pet**. At first we tied one of his legs to a tree to stop him from walking off, but after a time we let him go where he pleased. He enjoyed meal times and would sit in the sun while we gave him strawberries to eat. He loved sweet fruit, and strawberries were a special favourite. He also loved people. If you were sitting in a chair in the garden he used to go to sleep at your feet.

One sad day we found that Achilles had fallen down a deep hole in the ground. Although Leslie tried to breathe life into him, and Margo tried to bring him back to life by putting strawberries in

A tortoise

his mouth, he was clearly dead. With great seriousness we dug a hole under a strawberry plant in the garden (Mother's idea), and buried him there.

Not long after that, I bought a **pigeon** from the Rose-beetle

Man. It was still a very young bird at the time, and it had pink skin and only a few feathers, and was very fat. Larry said I should call him Quasimodo, and I did. Quasimodo didn't know how to fly, so he walked everywhere. If we went on a walk, he always wanted to come with us. This was boring because he walked slowly and made a lot of noise if we went too far in front, and if you picked him up and put him on your shoulder, there was always the danger of an accident to your clothes. He used to sleep at the end of Margo's bed until he began to sit on her face in the middle of the night. Then he was moved to the **sofa** in the sitting room. Quasimodo was a strange bird. It was Larry who discovered that he liked dancing to music. But the most surprising thing about Quasimodo was that one day we woke up to find him sitting on a white egg in the middle of the sofa. 'He' was a 'she'! After that she became more like a wild bird, and in the end she flew out of the house and went to live in the garden with the other pigeons.

A young pigeon

Soon after we had moved into the pink villa Mother decided I was becoming too wild and that I had to learn something. As usual everyone had their own ideas of what was important.

'I can teach him to shoot a gun, and if we buy a boat, I can teach him to sail,' said Leslie.

'He really must learn to dance,' said Margo.

'I think he should read the great writers of the past,' said Larry.

sofa a long soft seat for people to sit on together

'But what about French and **History** and **Mathematics**?' said Mother.

'Let me see,' said Larry. 'I suppose my friend George could teach him.'

'What a good idea!' said Mother. 'Will you speak to him? The sooner he starts the better.'

George was an old friend of Larry's who had come to Corfu to write. In fact he was the person who had given Larry the idea of us coming to live in Corfu in the first place.

He was tall and thin, and had a brown beard and thick glasses. He had a deep, sad voice and things made him laugh that no one else thought funny. So George began the job of teaching me French – using a French **dictionary**; introducing me to the great writers of the past – using his own books; and teaching me mathematics – using what he remembered from his own schooldays. But for me the most interesting lessons were George's natural history lessons. He taught me to look carefully at things and to write down what I had seen afterwards. I was happy to discover that when I wrote things down I could learn and remember more. Most mornings I arrived late for George's lessons, but I was always on time for his natural history lessons.

Together we used to sit in the sitting room of the villa with the green **shutters** on the windows closed against the sun.

'Let me see,' said George, looking seriously at his notes. 'We're supposed to be studying mathematics this morning.'

I stared at the boring problem on the page in front of me.

history the study of the past

mathematics the study of numbers

dictionary a book that gives words from A to Z, and explains what each word means

shutter a wooden thing that covers the outside of a window

How long will it take six men to build a wall if it takes three men a week to build it?

'Perhaps we can make it a little more interesting for you like this,' said George and he wrote a new problem out for me.

> If it takes two caterpillars a week to eat eight leaves, how long will four caterpillars take to eat the same number?

'Try that,' he said, and while I tried to answer the problem, George jumped round the dark sitting room walking through the steps of a village dance that he was busy trying to learn.

I liked **geography** lessons better. There I drew maps of the different countries with animals on them. And in my history lessons, George introduced some not very well known animal facts into the different stories to make things more interesting for me.

'Yes, the British sailors were getting ready to fight the French and they were a little worried by the large French ships all around them,' explained George. 'But when they saw their **captain**, Horatio Nelson, happily looking through his **collection** of seabirds' eggs they didn't feel so frightened.'

Quasimodo, my pet pigeon, used to come to my lessons until one day the stupid bird knocked green **ink** all over a beautiful map that I was drawing in my geography book. After that Quasimodo had to stay outside at lesson time. Achilles the tortoise had come to one lesson, but he got under the furniture and we had to move everything round to get him out, and after that he had to stay out during school hours too. In the end the only pet that could stay inside was Roger the dog, and he usually sat very quietly at my feet, unless he heard village dogs barking outside, and then he stood up and barked too.

Gerald and Roger, 1935

ACTIVITIES

READING CHECK

Match the first and second parts of these sentences.

a The Rose-beetle Man speaks by . . .

b Gerry makes friends with the
   Rose-beetle Man by . . .

c Achilles likes . . .

d Achilles is killed . . .

e Mother is worried about Gerry . . .

f Quasimodo isn't good at . . .

g Quasimodo likes . . .

h Everyone is surprised to find
   Quasimodo . . .

i Gerry loves . . .

j George believes in . . .

1 getting too wild.

2 eating strawberries.

3 moving his arms, face, mouth and
   eyes.

4 flying.

5 falling down a deep hole.

6 making his lessons as interesting as
   possible.

7 buying different animals from him.

8 sleeping on Margo's bed and dancing.

9 sitting on an egg one morning.

10 studying natural history.

WORD WORK

**Use the words in the pigeon to complete
Gerry's diary on page 25.**

captain collection
history dictionary
shutters Geography
sofa mathematics
tortoise feathers
shutters pigeon
pets
ink shutters

I have lots of **(a)** .....pets........ . I have a **(b)**........................... called Achilles. I also have a **(c)**.......................... called Quasimodo. He is young and he doesn't have many **(d)**......................... yet. I like **(e)**......................... because I like drawing maps. One day Quasimodo knocked green **(f)**......................... over one of them. I was very angry. I like learning about the past in my **(g)**......................... lessons. I loved the story about the British sea **(h)**......................... Horatio Nelson and his **(i)**......................... of seabirds' eggs. I hate numbers, so I don't enjoy my **(j)**......................... classes. And I don't really like French. I have to learn lots of words from George's **(k)**......................... . But my favourite time is when we close the green **(l)**......................... on the windows, sit down on the **(m)**......................... and I show George the insects I have found; my natural history lessons are great!

GUESS WHAT

What do you think happens in the next chapter? Tick the boxes. Yes No

a George gives Gerry some Greek dancing lessons. ☐ ☐

b Gerry finds new shells on the beach to add to his collection. ☐ ☐

c Gerry finds some interesting beetles. ☐ ☐

d Yani shows Gerry a dangerous animal in a bottle. ☐ ☐

e The Rose-beetle Man sells Gerry an interesting new pet. ☐ ☐

f Gerry makes friends with another person who likes natural history. ☐ ☐

CHAPTER 5

Scorpions and spiders

Sometimes George gave me lessons on the beach. I enjoyed swimming in the sea face down. Through the clear water I could see the brightly-coloured fish and the waving water plants that lay like an undersea forest below me. Sometimes I found new shells on the beach to add to my collection.

But best of all were the times when I could walk round the island on my own with Roger by my side. One hot dreamy afternoon when everyone except the cicadas seemed to be asleep, Roger and I went for a swim. Afterwards I lay on the beach until I was dry. Roger ran about in the water at the sea's edge until I called him. Then he came and shook himself near me, covering me with water from his thick coat.

Discovering I was hungry, I wondered which cottage to go to for something to eat. Before giving me food, Christaki the farmer and his family usually wanted to ask me lots of boring questions: *Is England bigger than Corfu? How many people live there? Are they all lords? What is a train like? Do trees grow in England?* I decided not to go there.

Instead I went to visit old Yani, the **shepherd**. He was sleeping on a chair outside his front door when I arrived, but when Roger began barking at the thin grey cat which was asleep under his chair, Yani soon woke up. The cat then ran off to safety.

shepherd a man who looks after sheep or goats

oil this is yellow and clear and comes from olives; you can cook things in it

scorpion a small animal with a long tail that has poison in it

'Aphrodite!' Yani called to his wife inside the cottage. 'Wake up! The little English lord is here. Bring us some food!'

While we were eating and drinking, he took a tiny bottle out of his pocket to show me.

'I caught him this morning,' he said. 'Hiding under a rock.'

He gave me the bottle to look at. It was full of **oil** and in the middle of the oil was a dead chocolate-brown **scorpion**.

'But why put him in oil?' I asked.

Yani laughed. 'When he dies in the oil, the **poison** comes out of his tail and makes a strong medicine. Then if one of his brothers bites you, you put some of this scorpion oil on the place and the poison in the bite doesn't hurt you.'

We talked for about an hour in this way, and then I got up. I thanked Yani and Aphrodite for their kindness, took the present of grapes that they offered me, and started back home, followed by Roger.

A scorpion

On the way home I sat down and ate my grapes with Roger, and it was then that I discovered something strange. The wall of **earth** behind me was covered in **moss**, and hidden in the moss were some little round doors as big as coins. I used a piece of grass to open one of these moss doors, and there was a hole going down into the earth behind it, but I could see nothing inside. What animal had made these doors? I wondered. And why?

I'll go and ask George about it, I thought. So, calling Roger, I ran off to George's villa.

'The fact that you hurried here happily tells me that you haven't come for extra lessons,' he said when I arrived.

I noticed then that someone was sitting in a chair near him. At first I thought he was George's brother. Like George, he had a beard. But unlike George, who was a very untidy man, the stranger was dressed in a fine grey suit, white shirt, dark tie and brown boots.

I turned back to George and explained to him about the little doors in the moss, and he turned to the man who was

poison something that kills people when they eat or drink it

earth the ground is made of this and plants grow in it

moss a soft green plant that grows like a carpet over the ground, trees or stones

visiting him and said; 'Theodore knows everything about natural history.'

'Well, I'm not sure I know everything!' said the man called Theodore, reddening.

'Gerry,' said George, 'can I introduce you? This is my friend, Doctor Theodore Stephanides. He is a nature lover like you.'

We shook hands.

'So Theodore,' George went on, 'what do you think made those strange secret doors in the moss?'

'Well . . . er . . .' he began, slowly and carefully. 'I believe that they are the work of the **trapdoor** spider. But of course, it is possible that I am making a mistake. Perhaps, if they are not too far away, we could go and look at them on my way home.'

Theodore

trapdoor a small secret door that can open suddenly

I told him that they were not far and he stood up and shook hands with George. 'Thank you for a very nice tea,' he said and, putting a fine grey hat on his head, he walked out of George's house and up the hill at my side.

When we reached the wall of moss he took out a small pocket-knife and opened one of the trapdoors with it.

'Ah, yes,' he said. 'This is the work of a trapdoor spider, but it's an old hole and there's no one at home. Usually the spider waits behind the door until a fly walks past, and then she jumps out and catches it. Most interesting!'

Afterwards we walked down the hill in silence. When we reached the road for the pink villa, I said goodbye.

'I have enjoyed meeting you,' Theodore said, looking down

A trapdoor spider

at his boots, and then he walked off home to town.

I hurried back to tell my family about my new discovery and my new friend. I couldn't wait to meet Theodore again. There were many things that I wanted to ask him.

Two days later, after a visit to town, Leslie gave me a packet.

'I met that doctor with the beard. He said this was for you,' he said.

I opened the packet. Inside there was a small box with a **microscope** in it and a letter.

My dear Gerry Durrell,
I am sending you this pocket microscope to help you with your natural history work on Corfu.
With best wishes,
Theodore Stephanides
PS If you're not busy on Thursday, please come to tea at my house.

In the end, I went to tea at Theodore's house every Thursday that summer. Spiro drove me there and I always took a number of insects that I had found that week to show to Theodore. We talked about the insects, and looked at them under his microscope. I could ask Theodore questions about anything and he always had an interesting answer for everything.

microscope
something with special glass in it that makes small things look much bigger

READING CHECK

Complete the sentences with the correct names.

Leslie   **George**   Spiro   Gerry

Theodore   Yani

a ...George...... gives Gerry lessons on the beach.

b .... feels hungry and goes to get food from a neighbour.

c .... asks his wife to bring things to eat and drink.

d .... shows Gerry a scorpion in a bottle.

e .... takes some grapes with him as a present.

f .... finds some strange holes in the ground on the way home.

g .... meets an interesting man at George's house.

h .... wears very nice clothes.

i .... is very untidy.

j .... goes with Gerry to look at the strange holes.

k .... gives Gerry a present from Theodore.

l .... takes Gerry to Theodore's house every Thursday.

Corfu harbour, 1930

WORD WORK

Match the words in the feathers with the correct definitions.

a something that makes very small things look a lot bigger .microscope.

b a small door that can open suddenly and is secret ....

c a plant that grows like a soft green carpet over things ....

d plants grow in this ....

e somebody who looks after sheep or goats ....

f something that makes you ill when it gets into your body ....

g a small animal that has a long tail with poison in it ....

h you can cook things in this; it is clear and yellow ....

earth
microscope
scorpion
shepherd
poison
trapdoor
oil
moss

GUESS WHAT

Match the first and second parts of these sentences to find out what happens in the next chapter.

a Mother invites Margo's new friend . . .

b The young man asks Margo . . .

c Leslie and Gerry go into the country . . .

d Larry invites some friends from England . . .

e Because they have lots of visitors the Durrells have . . .

f Mother finds a woman . . .

g Every Thursday Theodore comes . . .

1 to shoot birds one morning.

2 to go to the cinema one night.

3 to have tea at the pink villa.

4 to help with the housework.

5 to move to a bigger villa.

6 to look for insects with Gerry.

7 to stay for a week or two.

CHAPTER 6

How spring touched us

Autumn and winter came and went, and then it was spring. The smell of flowers filled the air, and the cypresses which had been thrown violently from side to side by the winter winds now stood tall and still against the clear spring sky.

Spring touched my family in different ways. Larry bought himself a guitar and when he wasn't writing, he played it,

Margo

Margo

and sang old English love songs in a high, weak voice. Mother liked spring, because it brought lots of vegetables for her to cook, and lots of bright flowers in the garden.

Margo became very strange in the spring. She changed and washed her clothes several times a day. She also hid for hours in the bathroom making herself look beautiful so that everyone got angry and knocked on the door and asked her to hurry up. Then she went down to the sea and swam.

It was on one of these visits to the beach that she made friends with a young man who was visiting Corfu on holiday. Spiro came to tell Mother all about it.

'What's the matter?' asked Mother seeing his worried face.

'It's Miss Margo,' said Spiro. 'Did you know she's meeting a man?'

'Yes, I did,' Mother lied.

'But she goes swimming with him. It's not safe!' said Spiro.

'I'll speak to Margo about it,' said Mother, and she told Margo to ask the young man for tea.

When he came, he was tall and handsome, with dark wavy hair. He kissed Mother's hand when he arrived and smiled coolly at the rest of us.

Mother gave him cakes and tea and tried to make conversation. The rest of us were silent. At last the handsome young man turned to Larry.

'I believe that you write,' he said, without much interest.

'Yes,' answered Larry, 'I do.'

'I have always felt I could write beautifully if I tried,' said the young man.

'Really?' said Mother.

'He swims well,' said Margo, 'and he goes out terribly far.'

'I have no fear,' said the young man fearlessly. 'I am an extraordinary swimmer, so I have no fear. When I ride a horse, I ride it beautifully because I have no fear. And I can sail a boat wonderfully in a storm without fear. I am not a fearful man,' he added.

He drank his tea and looked at our surprised faces with a pleased smile on his face.

The next day the young man sent a note to Margo asking her to go to the cinema with him.

So that evening Mother and Margo put on their best clothes and went off to the cinema. The film finished at ten o'clock but they didn't get back home until one in the morning.

'Oh, it was terrible,' said Mother, taking her shoes off.

'Awful,' agreed Margo.

'What happened?' asked Leslie.

'Well, to begin with he had lots of **perfume** on,' said Margo. 'I didn't like that.'

'And we had the cheapest seats at the cinema. They were too close to the front and I got a headache,' said Mother. 'And then on top of everything a **flea** jumped down my dress, and I couldn't get it out and it bit me everywhere. Later he bought us sweets and I began to feel terribly thirsty, and after that he bought us flowers.'

'But the worst part was coming home,' said Margo.

'Yes,' agreed Mother. 'It was a terrible journey. I thought we would come straight home by car, but he got a cab pulled by a horse and we had to drive round the town for hours while he sang love songs and smiled stupidly at Margo. And even when we got to the bottom of the hill he walked up with us carrying a big stick, because he said the forest was full of **snakes** at this time of year. I was so glad when he went. I'm afraid that you must choose your boyfriends more carefully in future, Margo. I don't want to have another night like that again, dear.'

Leslie saw spring as a good time to get out his guns and shoot wood pigeons. I remember one time when he and I went out together at first light and he killed five birds in less than an hour.

After that, on our way home, we met Yani the shepherd who was taking his goats out for the day. His brown face smiled at us and he lifted his hand in the air to say hello. '*Chairete!*' he called out in Greek. 'Be happy!'

The goats moved amongst the olive trees, their bells ringing, and the island stood wet and bright in the morning sun. Be happy! How could you feel any other way during the spring?

As soon as we were at home on the island, Larry wrote to all his friends and asked them to come and visit us.

perfume something with a nice smell that you put on your skin

flea a very small insect that can jump; it lives on and bites animals and people

snake a long animal with no legs

34

'I've asked a few people to visit us for a week or two,' he told Mother one morning.

'That's nice,' she replied carelessly. 'We must tell the hotel in town when they're coming.'

'The hotel?' asked Larry, surprised.

'Yes, so they can keep rooms for them,' said Mother, also surprised.

'But I've asked them to stay here,' Larry explained.

'Larry! You haven't! You really are thoughtless. How can they stay here? The villa's too small to have people to stay.'

'Then we must move to a bigger villa.'

'Don't be silly! How many people have you invited, by the way?'

'Oh, seven or eight.'

'But that makes thirteen with ourselves! That's too many to fit into this villa.'

'So let's move.'

'We are not moving to another villa!' said Mother. 'And that's final.'

The new villa was very big. It had bright yellow walls, green shutters and a red roof, and it stood high on a hill above the sea with orange trees and vines all around it. It was Spiro of course who found the place for us, and who helped us to move all our things there. There was a little cottage at the bottom of the garden where the old gardener and his wife lived. In a moment of unthinking kindness Mother asked the gardener's wife to come and work for us in the villa. Her name was Lugaretzia. She was a thin woman with a long sad face whose long hair never stayed tidy for long. Lugaretzia used to cry if you said anything bad about her work, so Mother learnt to leave her to do the job in her own way. The only thing that made Lugaretzia happy was talking about her aches and pains, which she did even when nobody wanted to listen.

Apart from Lugaretzia, the other problem in the yellow villa was the furniture. It was all so old that it fell to pieces when you touched it.

'We can't have people to stay when everything is falling to pieces,' said Mother.

So Spiro had to drive Mother, Margo and myself into town to buy new furniture.

'Really,' said Mother, 'these visitors are going to be the most expensive we've ever had!'

I was very happy looking round the garden of the new house. Larry's friend George had left the island and I was without a teacher for a time. I could spend the whole day outside, only going back to the villa for meals. I felt as free as a bird! I found many old friends in this new garden – rose-beetles, ladybirds, and trapdoor spiders. There were also shiny black scorpions, green lizards and earth-coloured tortoises to amuse me.

Now that spring was in the air Theodore came up to our villa every Thursday for tea. He came from the town in a cab pulled by two horses, and his fine suit and hat looked very strange next to the butterfly nets, jars and boxes that he brought with him. Before tea we **examined** the new insects I had found, and Theodore **identified** them for me. After tea we looked for new insects together in the garden.

Not long after we had arrived at the yellow villa, I discovered that the hills behind the house belonged to a number of tortoises. I have never seen so many in one place. One day, in just two hours, I picked up and looked at thirty-five different animals as they walked past me. Amongst them there was a large **female** with only one eye that I got to know well. I called her Madam Cyclops. I brought her leaves to eat and she learnt not to be afraid of me. One day I got very excited when I found her burying nine white tortoise eggs in the ground. I

examine to look carefully at something

identify to say what something is by name

female an animal that can make eggs or have babies

Outside the yellow villa, 1936

took one of them when she wasn't looking, and brought it back to the villa. There I made two tiny holes in opposite ends of the egg and blew into one of them to take out the inside. Afterwards that egg had a special place in my natural history collection. I put it in a little glass box, and wrote a beautiful **label** for it in black ink that said 'Madam Cyclops's egg'.

All through the spring and summer, Larry's friends came to stay with us. They were a strange group of writers and artists. I remember the first was Zatopec, an Armenian writer. He was short and fat, and had long grey hair, a long black coat, and a big black hat. He never stopped talking all the time that he was with us. He was very old but still crazy about women. He was very polite to Mother and Margo of course, but he used to run laughing through the fields after all the village girls and tell them that he loved them.

When Zatopec went, we were visited by Jonquil – a funny young **artist** from East London.

'I 'aven't come 'ere on 'oliday!' she said when she arrived. 'I came to work.'

And then she lay out in the garden in a swimsuit and slept calmly in the sun every day of her stay.

label a piece of paper or cloth that you fix to something to give information about it

artist a person who makes pictures

ACTIVITIES

READING CHECK

Correct the mistakes in these sentences.

a The whole family are happy when ~~autumn~~ *spring* comes.

b Mother is worried because Margo is meeting a man at the beach.

c Margo's boyfriend isn't very pleased with himself.

d Mother and the Durrell boys like Margo's boyfriend very much.

e Larry invites his friends to stay at the hotel.

f The Durrells move to a smaller villa.

g They have to buy paint for the villa.

h Lugaretzia, the gardener's wife, helps Mother in the garden.

i Gerry is happy because Theodore has left the island.

j Gerry gets a pigeon egg for his natural history collection.

WORD WORK

Find words in the tortoises to complete the sentences.

a Mother is badly bitten by a f l e a at the cinema.

b Margo's boyfriend wears lots of p _ _ _ _ _ _ when they go to the cinema.

c A stick is good for hitting s _ _ _ _ _ with if they attack you.

d Gerry takes one of Madam Cyclops's eggs; she is a large f _ _ _ _ _ tortoise with one eye.

e Theodore knows a lot about insects and can i _ _ _ _ _ _ _ _ them easily.

f Using the microscope Gerry and Theodore e _ _ _ _ _ _ _ the insects that Gerry has found.

g Gerry writes l _ _ _ _ _ _ in black ink for the things in his collection.

h Jonquil is a funny a _ _ _ _ _ from East London.

e a m e l

y d n i t e f

x i n e m a

a b s e l

t t r s i

GUESS WHAT

What happens in the next chapter? Match the photographs and the sentences.

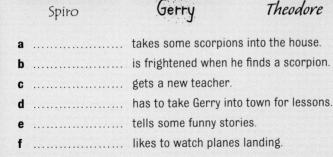

Spiro   Gerry   Theodore   Larry

a .... takes some scorpions into the house.

b .... is frightened when he finds a scorpion.

c .... gets a new teacher.

d .... has to take Gerry into town for lessons.

e .... tells some funny stories.

f .... likes to watch planes landing.

CHAPTER 7

A matchbox and a plane

The old wall around the garden at the side of the house was a good place to look for animals. It was covered in moss and had lots of **cracks** between its stones. The animals that lived there were of different kinds. Some were day workers, some were night workers, some were killers, and some were food.

A gecko

At night the killers were the **geckos** who lived in the cracks high up on the wall. They were **pale** and thin-skinned and had big round eyes. Every night they ate the **moths** that flew near the wall, and the beetles that walked importantly across its dark stones.

In the day it was more difficult to identify who was the food and who were the killers. The spiders ate flies. Some of the bigger insects ate spiders and flies. And the big brightly-coloured wall lizards ate everything.

But the quietest of the animals on that wall were the most dangerous. When you put a knife into the wall and made a hole, there was always a little scorpion hiding in there, looking dark-brown and shiny like something made of chocolate. They didn't hurt you if you were careful, and I loved watching them and putting them in jars so that I could see how they moved their legs. They ate flies, moths and other small insects. Sometimes they even ate other scorpions, which I thought wasn't very nice of them.

Although I really wanted to study scorpions more closely, my family had told me that I couldn't bring any of them inside

crack a deep line where something is broken in two parts

gecko a small light-coloured lizard that wakes up at night; it can run up and down walls

pale without a lot of colour

moth a kind of butterfly that flies at night; they often fly towards the light

the house. Then one day I found a fat female scorpion in the wall. At first I thought she was wearing a kind of pale brown coat, but when I looked closer I saw that she had lots of tiny babies riding on her back. I fell in love with this scorpion family at once and decided to take them back home and up to my bedroom where I could keep them and watch them grow bigger.

With great care I got mother and babies into a matchbox and then hurried into the villa. When I entered the house, lunch was ready, so I left my matchbox on the table in the front room and ate with the rest of the family.

After the meal I stayed in my chair. I gave Roger something to eat under the table, and listened to the family arguing. I forgot all about my exciting new discovery. Larry finished his meal and went into the front room to get his cigarettes. He came back, sat down in his chair, put a cigarette in his mouth and then opened the matchbox that he had brought with him.

A mother scorpion carrying babies

Now I'm sure that the female scorpion didn't want to hurt anyone. She was worried and angry at being shut up in a matchbox, and she jumped at the first chance of escape. She ran out of the box and up Larry's hand with her babies on her back and then stopped, her tail held dangerously high in the air, unsure of what to do next. Larry felt her running over his skin and looked down, and from that moment everything went crazy.

He gave a cry of fear, Lugaretzia dropped a plate on the floor, and Roger came out from under the table barking wildly. Then Larry threw the scorpion onto the table. She landed between Margo and Leslie, and her babies fell off all over the place. Then she ran towards Leslie. Leslie jumped up from his chair and knocked her away with a **napkin**. Now she ran towards Margo who screamed like a railway engine. Mother who couldn't understand why everyone was shouting and jumping up and down, put on her glasses and looked at the table to see what was making them act so strangely.

At that moment Margo decided to throw a glass of water at the scorpion but missed the animal and threw the cold water over Mother by mistake. Mother sat down in surprise and couldn't say a thing for some time, and the scorpion hid under Leslie's plate while her babies ran all over the table.

'It's that boy again!' shouted Larry.

'Look out! They're coming!' screamed Margo.

'Quick! Get a book and hit them!' cried Leslie. 'And be quiet Roger!'

'What is the matter with you all?' asked Mother when she could speak again.

'It's Gerry. He'll kill us. Scorpions all over the table!'

'But how did they get there?'

'In the matchbox!'

While all this was going on Roger ran about barking. He felt that something was **attacking** the family and because the

napkin you use this to cover your clothes and to clean your mouth while you are eating

attack to start fighting

only stranger in the room was Lugaretzia, he bit her on the leg. This did not make things any better at all.

In the end all the baby scorpions hid under plates, knives, forks and spoons and things became calmer. The rest of the family went into the front room while I picked up all the babies with a teaspoon and put them on their mother's back. Then I put her on a plate and took her out into the garden and left her on the wall that she'd come from in the first place. Then I went for a long walk in the country with Roger, and the rest of the family went off for their **siestas**. I didn't come back home until long after siesta time.

After that day Larry became frightened of matchboxes and was always very careful when he lit a cigarette. Lugaretzia walked around the house for weeks with a **bandage** on her leg talking about how her poor leg was slowly getting better. And Mother decided it was time that I had another teacher to stop me from being so wild.

So I went to have French lessons from a little Belgian man in the town. Spiro took me down every morning. The Belgian was a cat lover and he made me read from a French dictionary and told me how to say the words when I made mistakes. I was very bored, and sadly I didn't learn very much French, but my morning lessons really made me enjoy my afternoon walks in the country even more than usual. And of course there was always Thursday, when Theodore came up to the villa just after lunch and stayed until the moon was high in the night sky.

It was lucky that Theodore came on a Thursday because this was the day that the sea-plane arrived from Athens, flew over our house, and landed in the sea nearby. Theodore loved watching sea-planes land, but if you wanted to see it clearly you had to go up to the **attic** and put your head out of the window.

siesta a short rest or sleep that people take in the afternoon in hot countries

bandage a long thin cloth that you tie round part of your body when you have hurt it

attic a little room at the top of a house

A sea-plane, 1938

The plane almost always arrived in the middle of tea. At first it sounded like a flying insect far away. Theodore used to stop in the middle of a funny story he was telling and listen carefully, his head on one side.

'Is that . . . er . . . you know . . . the noise of a plane?'

Then when it got nearer, he used to say, 'Yes, I'm sure it is a plane!' After that, Mother spoke.

'Would you like to go up and see it land?' she asked.

And Theodore always replied, 'Yes . . . er . . . I find it so beautiful . . . if you don't mind.'

The plane now was right above us, and we all shouted together, 'Hurry up Theo, or you'll miss it.'

Then we all ran upstairs with Theodore and Roger to the attic and watched the plane land in the sea.

Afterwards Theodore always said, 'Erm . . . yes . . . that was lovely!' And we closed the window and went noisily downstairs again and finished our tea. The next week we did the same thing all over again.

Thursdays were also when Theodore and I went on our natural history walks. Sometimes we stayed in the garden and sometimes we went out into the fields, the hills and the mountains. Carrying our boxes and nets, we walked through the olive trees and Roger ran in front of us, his nose to the ground. During these Thursday walks I discovered that Theodore knew lots about almost everything, but he told you about it in a really nice way. It was more like someone helping you to remember facts that you had forgotten than someone who was teaching you something new. He also loved telling funny stories.

'Did I tell you what happened to a friend of mine? He needed a new floor on the top of his house – with bedrooms and bathrooms and everything – and he decided to build it himself. Well, when it was finished, the builders took away their **ladders** and he had a party for all his friends. But when one of them wanted to visit the new floor, the man discovered that the only way up and down had been by using the builders' ladders because he'd forgotten to put in any stairs.'

In this way we walked though the hot afternoon, stopping by lakes and rivers, travelling along white earth roads where sometimes we met a sleepy man on his donkey going home for a rest. Towards evening we went back home carrying our jars, bottles and nets full of strange and exciting animals. The sky was gold, as we walked through the dark lines of olive trees, and the air was cooler and full of the rich smells of flowers, plants, and trees. Roger used to run in front of us, sometimes looking back over his shoulder to see that we were following him. And Theodore and I, tired and dirty, our heavy bags making our shoulders ache pleasantly, sang songs to keep our feet moving as we walked back to the villa.

Theodore loved telling funny stories

ladder you use this for climbing up or down tall buildings or other things

READING CHECK

1 Put these sentences in order. Number them 1–8.

a ☐ Gerry puts the scorpions into a matchbox.

b ☐ Roger is worried by the noise and bites Lugaretzia's leg.

c ☐ Leslie tries to hit the scorpion and it runs towards Margo, who screams.

d ☐ Gerry finds a mother scorpion with some babies on her back.

e ☐ Margo throws a glass of water over Mother by mistake.

f ☐ Larry opens the box, and the scorpion runs up his hand.

g ☐ The scorpion falls on the table and runs towards Leslie.

h ☐ Gerry goes for a long walk with Roger.

2 Are these sentences true or false? Tick the boxes.

	True	False
a Gerry's new teacher is French.	☐	☑
b This new teacher likes dogs.	☐	☐
c Gerry doesn't enjoy his morning lessons.	☐	☐
d Theodore comes to lunch on Thursdays.	☐	☐
e Theodore likes watching the sea-plane land.	☐	☐
f Theodore and Gerry go on natural history walks on Thursdays.	☐	☐
g Theodore loves telling Gerry sad stories.	☐	☐

WORD WORK

Find words in the puzzle to complete the sentences on page 47.

c r a c	p a	g e c	t h s
b a n	n a p k	s i	~~k s~~
m o	e s t a	a c k	t i c
a t t	k o s	a t	l e
d e r	d a g e	i n	l a d

ACTIVITIES

a The old garden wall at the side of the yellow house has ......cracks...... between its stones.

b People who live in hot countries often take a .... after lunch.

c Theodore goes up to the .... at the top of the house to see the sea-plane land.

d .... fly towards lights at night.

e .... run about over walls at night and eat insects.

f Leslie uses his .... to knock the mother scorpion away.

g Roger bites Lugaretzia because he thinks she wants to .... the family.

h For many weeks Lugaretzia walks around with a .... on her leg.

i A man who built his house with no stairs had to use a builder's .... to go upstairs.

j The baby scorpions are .... brown.

GUESS WHAT

What do you think happens in the next chapter? Tick the boxes.   Yes   No

a A new teacher from England arrives for Gerry.

b Larry meets a beautiful young woman.

c Gerry starts writing a book.

d Margo becomes interested in Gerry's new teacher.

e The Durrells move house again.

f Spiro asks Mother to marry him.

g Gerry gets a new pet.

h The family go out dancing on summer nights.

CHAPTER 8

Swimming by moonlight

Spring changed slowly into the long hot sunny days of summer and the cicadas sang loudly all over the island. The grapes lay warm and yellow on the vines, the olives sat heavy on the branches of the olive trees like bright green stones, and on the orange trees the once green fruit began to shine like bright orange lamps amongst the dark-green leaves.

Up on the hills the butterflies danced in the sun, stopping from time to time to land on a leaf and leave their eggs there. In the evening, when the sun went down, the light of day became a green half-light that in the end changed to a pale purple. Then it grew cooler, the cicadas fell silent, and the geckos came out, hungry for moths and other night insects. The sea was still, warm and dark as a fine black sheet, and when the moon climbed up, red as blood over the mountains and into the sky, she threw a straight road of red light across the dark waters below her. The **owls** came out now, flying from tree to tree silently, and calling out in surprise as the moon climbed higher and higher and changed from pink to gold, and finally came to rest among the stars like a tiny silver ball of light.

That summer Peter, a new teacher from England, arrived. He was a tall, handsome young man who had just left Oxford University. He had clear ideas about what teaching meant, which I didn't like at first. But slowly life on the island changed him and he took things more easily. Instead of giving me mathematics problems and boring English lessons inside the house, he went swimming with me and asked me to write things which he could correct later.

So I began to write a book and every morning I wrote a

owl a bird with large eyes that flies at night and eats small animals

Margo

chapter of it. It was an adventure story about my family going on a journey round the world and it had lots of different animals in it. Each chapter ended at an exciting part of the story – with a big wild cat running towards Mother, or Larry fighting a large snake. While I was writing, Peter and Margo used to walk off round the garden together. I was surprised that they had both suddenly become so interested in garden plants. In this way the mornings went by very pleasantly for all of us. At first Peter sometimes felt that he was not doing his job of teaching me very well, and I had to put my adventure book away and look at mathematics problems instead. But as the summer days grew longer, and Margo became more and more interested in garden plants, this happened less and less often.

After the time that the scorpion had escaped from the matchbox, I was given a big room on the first floor for all my animals to go in. I called it my **study**, but the rest of the family called it the **bug** room. Here I kept my natural history books, my diary, my microscope, my butterfly nets, my bottles, jars and other important things. I had several large boxes full of my collections of birds' eggs, beetles, and butterflies – all with carefully written labels describing what they contained. And sitting in **alcohol** in some large jars, I kept a number of interesting things like a chicken with four legs (a present from Lugaretzia's husband), different lizards and snakes, and a tiny baby tortoise which had died one winter.

I was always looking for new animals to add to my collection. One day, when I was climbing an olive tree, I put my arm into a hole, and my fingers closed on something small and soft hiding inside. It was something that tried to escape from my hand as I pulled it out. When my hand was free of the tree, I looked down and found that it held a little baby owl. He at once bit my thumb angrily and we both fell off the branch that I was holding onto and landed on the hard earth below. Luckily the angry little owl was unhurt and I carried him back home in my pocket. There I introduced him, worried but hopeful, to my family. To my surprise none of them said that I couldn't keep him. So he came to live in a **basket** in my study and was given the name Ulysses.

From the start, even when he was small enough to fit in a teacup, Ulysses was a fearless bird. Soon after he had come to stay with us, I put him on the floor and tried to get Roger to come and make friends with him. But when Roger got close, Ulysses jumped on his black nose and dug his knife-like **claws** deep into it. This made Roger bark and run away at once. He went and hid under the table and didn't want to come out again until I had put Ulysses safely back in his basket.

When Ulysses grew older he got too big for his basket and

study a room in a house where you go to write or work

bug a small insect

alcohol this keeps things from going bad; it is also found in beer and wine

basket a container that is usually made of thin pieces of wood

claw a sharp thing on a bird's or an animal's foot that they use to fight with

Gerald (aged 11)
with Ulysses

I let him move freely round my study. He took flying lessons by jumping from the table over to the door **handle** and back again. Once he could fly well, he used to sleep on top of a cupboard during the day. He woke up when the sun went down and the geckos came out and began to run across the dark walls of the house. He shook his wings, cleaned his tail, and then flew down onto my shoulder and bit my ear gently and playfully. Then he shook himself again and flew across to the study window and looked at me with his round yellow eyes. Once I had opened the shutters, he stood for a moment black against the white moon. Then he flew out into the night, calling *Tywhoo! Tywhoo!* as a warning cry as he began to look for food amongst the dark olive trees.

handle you move this to open a door or pull out a drawer

beak the hard
pointed part of a
bird's mouth

row to move a
boat through water
using long pieces
of wood with flat
ends

Ulysses always came back home between nine and ten for his supper. If there was no light in my study he flew down to the kitchen, and if I wasn't there he flew up to my bedroom. He used to knock with his **beak** on the shutters if they were closed to tell me to open them. His supper was a plate of meat or a chicken's heart which I had carefully cut into little pieces for him. After he had eaten, he sat still as if thinking deep thoughts for a moment and then flew out once more into the night sky, sailing high and silent over the moon-bright tree tops.

Once Ulysses had shown Roger that he was a fearless fighter, the two of them became more friendly. Sometimes Ulysses came with us when we went for a late evening swim. He used to ride down to the beach on Roger's back. If Roger forgot about him and went too fast or jumped over a rock, Ulysses stared at him angrily with round yellow eyes, opening and closing his beak and moving his wings restlessly. When Roger and I went into the sea Ulysses used to sit on my clothes on the beach and wait for us to finish. And if we spent longer than usual in the water, he used to fly back up the hill to the garden crying *Tywhoo!* as his way of saying goodbye.

During the summer, when the moon was full, the family often used to go swimming at night, because the beach was too hot during the day. When the moon climbed up into the sky we went down to the beach, and climbed into our little boat the *Sea Cow*. Larry, Leslie, Margo and Peter **rowed** the boat down the coast while Roger and I sat at the front to see where we were going, ready to call 'Look out!' if we saw any rocks in our way. Once

Leslie and friend on the Sea Cow

we had reached deeper waters, we jumped into the warm sea and swam about there happily. When we felt tired, we swam to a nearby beach and lay on the warm flat rocks looking up at the starry sky and talking.

porpoise a friendly, intelligent sea animal that breathes air

After about half an hour I usually got bored with the conversation, went back into the sea, and swam out again to deep water where I lay on my back looking up at the moon. I could hear the others, laughing and talking on the rocks. Suddenly I felt something moving in the dark waters around me. What kind of animal was it? I felt worried and had just decided that I should shout for help. Then I saw a dark shiny back swim past me and I heard the gentle noise of breathing as the back came out of the water for a moment and then went under again. I just had time to recognize that it was a **porpoise**, when I suddenly realized that I was swimming in the middle of a group of porpoises. They were swimming all around me, coming up for air, their black backs shining in the moonlight. There were about eight or nine of them and they seemed to love playing in the water. I swam with them for a while, watching them with great interest, until at last they turned and swam off together towards Albania. I stayed in the water and watched them go, swimming and jumping playfully in and out of the sea, which lay as warm and white as a road of milk before them.

A porpoise

READING CHECK

Choose the right words to finish these sentences.

a This chapter takes place in . . .
   1 ☐ autumn.
   2 ☐ spring.
   3 ☑ summer.

b Gerry starts writing . . .
   1 ☐ a nature diary.
   2 ☐ an adventure story.
   3 ☐ a love story for Margo.

c Gerry's new teacher . . .
   1 ☐ has just left school.
   2 ☐ likes giving mathematics lessons.
   3 ☐ is very interested in Margo.

d Gerry finds a small bird . . .
   1 ☐ when he is looking for scorpions.
   2 ☐ in a hole in a tree.
   3 ☐ but his family don't like it.

e Ulysses and Roger . . .
   1 ☐ don't like each other at all.
   2 ☐ always have fights.
   3 ☐ become friendly in the end.

f Ulysess . . .
   1 ☐ goes everywhere with Gerry and Roger.
   2 ☐ never leaves the house.
   3 ☐ isn't good at finding his own food.

g One night Gerry swims with . . .
   1 ☐ Ulysses.
   2 ☐ Mother and the rest of the family.
   3 ☐ some playful animals.

ACTIVITIES

WORD WORK

Use the definitions to complete the crossword puzzle.

a you can open and close a door with this

b a bird's mouth

c something sharp on a bird's or an animal's foot

d a friendly sea animal that breathes air

e you can find this in beer and wine

f to move a boat through water

g Gerry's pet Ulysses is one of these birds

h a room where you can write or work quietly

i you can carry things in this

j small insects

Crossword grid with answer 'a' spelled HANDLE and 'b' BA_ _

GUESS WHAT

Make four sentences with these phrases to find out what happens in the next chapter.

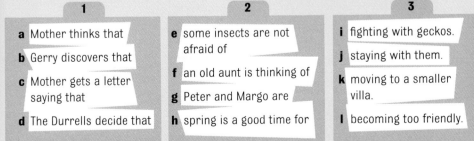

1

a Mother thinks that

b Gerry discovers that

c Mother gets a letter saying that

d The Durrells decide that

2

e some insects are not afraid of

f an old aunt is thinking of

g Peter and Margo are

h spring is a good time for

3

i fighting with geckos.

j staying with them.

k moving to a smaller villa.

l becoming too friendly.

CHAPTER 9

The great fight

That autumn, I found myself again without a teacher. Mother had discovered that Margo and Peter were becoming 'too close', and one night Peter was sent away. I was very pleased about Peter leaving, but poor Margo couldn't stop crying. A little while later she got a note from him saying he would come back for her. Margo got worried, and showed the note to Mother. After that Spiro watched the boats that arrived on the island very carefully. Leslie got out his guns to shoot Peter if he arrived at the house. Larry was telling Margo to run off with Peter one day, and the next day he was telling her to stop crying all the time. Margo went and hid in the attic for a week, red-eyed and reading love **poetry**, and I took her large meals there, which she ate hungrily.

When spring came, Mother got a long letter from Great Aunt Hermione.

'She says that the doctors aren't very hopeful that she'll get better,' Mother told us.

'They've said that for forty years,' said Larry, 'and she's still alive.'

'She says that she was surprised when we ran off to Corfu, but that they've had a very bad winter in England. Now she's beginning to think that it was wise of us to choose a healthy place to live in . . . and . . . oh, no!'

'What's the matter?'

'She says she wants to come and stay with us. The doctors have told her that she needs some warm weather for a while.'

'She can't come!' cried Larry. 'It's bad enough listening to Lugaretzia talking about her aches and pains all the time, without having Great Aunt Hermione busy dying all over the

poetry short pieces of careful writing; it is often about what you feel

place. You'll have to tell her that we haven't got room.'

'I can't do that!' said Mother. 'I told her in my last letter what a big villa we have.'

'She's probably forgotten.'

'No, she hasn't. She writes here: "You say that you have a large villa and I am sure that you wouldn't mind an old lady who has not got much longer to live coming to stay in a small corner of it." There you are! What can we do?'

'Why don't we say we're all terribly ill?'

'We can't do that! I've told her how healthy it is here.'

'Then there's only one thing left to do,' said Larry.

'What's that, dear?' asked Mother, looking over her glasses at him.

'We must move to a smaller villa. Then you can write and tell Great Aunt Hermione that we really haven't got room for her.'

'Don't be stupid, Larry. We can't go on moving from villa to villa. People will think we're crazy.'

'They'll think we're even crazier if Great Aunt Hermione comes to stay.'

And so we moved.

The snow-white villa stood on top of a hill with olive trees all around it. A grape vine grew all along one side of it and there was a tiny walled garden at the front of it. We liked it as soon as Spiro showed it to us.

It was at the white villa that I really got to know insects of the **praying mantis** family. They climbed up the different trees around the garden and

praying mantis a big green insect with a long body, small triangular head and strong front legs that eats other smaller insects

The snow-white villa today

57

at night they flew into the house, the lamplight shining on their green wings which moved like the wheels of an old **paddle steamer**. They landed on chairs and tables and walked about on their long thin legs, turning their heads from side to side looking for smaller bugs to eat, and staring at us from round black eyes in triangular faces. Some of them were as big as your hand.

Praying mantises

These insects seemed to think the house belonged to them, and so did the geckos that lived there. The two animal groups often fought together. There were lots of smaller fights between the geckos and the mantises that weren't very interesting, but I was lucky enough to see one of the really big fights because it actually happened in my bedroom. There was one gecko who lived in my bedroom that I liked a lot. I called him Geronimo, after the Indian chief, because he seemed a fearless and clever animal.

Most of the mantises that flew into my room at night were small things. Geronimo often ran across the **ceiling** or down the wall towards them, but they were too quick for him and always flew away before he could catch them.

The night of the great fight was different. That night Geronimo met a mantis who not only refused to run away, but actually went to meet him.

paddle steamer a ship that is driven by an engine and is moved forwards by large wheels

ceiling the part of a room above your head

sharp that can cut or make holes like a knife

For a long time I had wanted to get hold of some mantis eggs and one day I saw a large female mantis outside in the hills. Her stomach was very round and large and it was clear that she was carrying eggs. I went to pick her up but she got angry and hurt my fingers and thumbs with her **sharp** front claws. I picked her up very carefully, took her home with me, put her in a box in my bedroom, and called her Cicely. I caught lots of butterflies for her with my net and she ate them hungrily and her stomach got bigger and bigger. But one night she found a hole in her box and escaped.

I was sitting and reading in bed when Cicely suddenly flew across the room and landed on the wall not far from Geronimo the gecko. He had just finished a meal of moth and he looked over at Cicely in surprise. She was bigger than he was. For some time Geronimo looked at Cicely, and Cicely looked around and pretended not to see Geronimo at all.

Then Geronimo suddenly moved forwards, his tail waving angrily, and at once Cicely turned to face him, stood up on her back legs, opened her wings wide, and lifted her sharp front legs up in the air, ready to attack.

Geronimo stopped for a moment. Then he ran again towards her and bit her hard on the chest. At the same time her sharp front claws closed on his back legs. For some time they fought like this, each trying to get the better of the other. Cicely wanted to pull Geronimo down to the floor, and Geronimo wanted to pull Cicely up to the ceiling.

Then Cicely made a terrible mistake. She tried to fly away across the room. But Geronimo was heavy and her wings weren't strong enough to lift them both. They fell together down onto the bed.

I was going to stop the fight at that moment but then Geronimo got one of Cicely's sharp front legs in his mouth and she put her other claw round his neck. They began to walk up the blanket locked together like this and I got out of bed. I didn't want to get one of Cicely's claws in my neck or chest.

Both animals were now seriously hurt. One of Cicely's wings was torn and one of her back legs was broken and useless. Geronimo had cuts across his back and neck from Cicely's sharp claws.

Now Cicely made her second big mistake. She let Geronimo's

neck go free and put her claw round his tail instead.

As soon as her claws dug into his tail it fell off, and Geronimo bit off Cicely's other arm. Cicely was busy watching Geronimo's tail waving from one side to the other in her claw and she didn't see Geronimo's next move. The gecko jumped forwards and his mouth closed on the mantis's head and neck, and he refused to open it again. After a short while Cicely stopped moving and that was the end of the fight. I caught five fat flies and gave them to Geronimo afterwards as a present, and he ate them gratefully.

My other discovery at that time was two great **toads** that I found under a fallen olive tree in a valley to the left of the white villa. They were fat, as big as plates, and greeny-grey in colour with white spots here and there on their bodies, and yellow eyes. I took them at once to show to Mother and Spiro who were busy putting shopping away into the cupboard in the kitchen.

When Spiro saw the two toads in my hands, his face suddenly changed colour to a toad-like green, and he ran out into the garden and **was** violently **sick**.

'You mustn't show Spiro things like that, dear,' said Mother. 'You know that he's got a weak stomach.'

'But what's wrong with them?' I asked looking down at the two toad brothers lovingly.

'There's nothing wrong with them, dear,' said Mother bravely. 'They're lovely. It's just that not everyone likes them.'

The rest of the family felt the same about the toads as Spiro did, and so I took them away and put them in a box under my bed.

Next Thursday, when Theodore came to visit, I brought my toads down for him to examine and identify, and he was very interested in them. He took one brother out of the box and put it on the floor.

toad a small fat animal with strong back legs that can jump well; it can live on land or in the water

be sick to bring food up from your stomach and out of your mouth

'Aha! Yes, they are two very fine garden toads, as you say.'

'How old are they?' I asked him.

He picked the other toad up and put that on the floor next to his brother.

'Well, it's hard to say, but I imagine they're about twelve or even twenty years old!'

And then he went and dug a large **worm** out of the earth in the garden. He brought it back into the room and put it on the floor in front of the two toads. Then we both sat and watched with interest as the nearest toad caught the worm with its tongue and slowly ate it, bit by bit, just like someone eating spaghetti.

worm a small long pink animal with no legs that lives in the earth

A garden toad

READING CHECK

Use the names to complete the chapter summary.

Aunt Hermione | Cicely | Geronimo | Gerry | Leslie | Margo | Peter | Larry

(a) .....Peter....... is sent away because he is becoming too friendly with
(b) .... **(c)** .... can't stop crying when he goes.
(d) .... says he's going to shoot **(e)** .... if he comes
back. When a letter arrives from **(f)** .... asking to come and stay,
(g) .... says they must move to a smaller villa. In the smaller white villa
(h) .... sees a fight one night between **(i)** ...., a gecko,
and **(j)** ...., a large praying mantis that has escaped from her box.
(k) .... wins the fight and **(l)** .... dies at the end of it.

WORD WORK

1 Find words from Chapter 9 in the trapdoor.

2 **Use words from Activity 1 to complete the sentences.**

a Cicely is a very big ..... praying ... . mantis ....

b Cicely has very .... front claws.

c When Cicely flies across the room her wings move like the wheels of a

....

d Geckos have special feet and can walk across the ....

e Gerry finds two big .... under a fallen olive tree.

f Spiro's face goes green and he runs into the garden to ....

....

g Theodore examines Gerry's new pets and gets a .... for them to eat.

h Margo reads lots of love .... when she is thinking about Peter.

GUESS WHAT

What do you think happens in the next chapter? Tick the boxes.   **Yes**   **No**

a Gerry makes friends with a murderer.   ☐   ☐

b Gerry gets a new bird to look after.   ☐   ☐

c Mother decides to leave Corfu and go back to England.   ☐   ☐

d The children are happy to return to England.   ☐   ☐

e Spiro goes to England with the Durrell family.   ☐   ☐

A terrapin

CHAPTER 10

How it all ended

Below the villa, on the flat land between the hills that the villa stood on and the sea, were the **chessboard** fields. These were small square fields of different colours which had **canals** running between them from the old days when the people on the island used them to make salt from the sea water. Most of the fields belonged to friends of mine, and each had a fruit or vegetable garden on it. They were the perfect place for getting the latest island news. They were also a favourite place of mine to look for new animals.

One afternoon, when I had nothing better to do, I went down to the chessboard fields to try to catch Old Plop. Old Plop was a big old **terrapin** that lived on one of the canals. I had wanted to catch him for some months, but although he was old, he was clever and quick. Every time I walked up quietly towards him, when he was sleeping in the sun on the **mud** at the side of one of the canals, he always heard me, and woke up. Before my eyes he threw himself down a mud **slide** into the water and disappeared.

On this day I didn't find Old Plop, but I did find two fat brown water snakes, a **male** and a female, **mating** on the grassy mud by one of the canals. I quickly picked up a stick to catch the snakes with, but how could I catch two snakes with one stick? Then, as fast as a knife, the male snake threw himself down a mud slide into the water. At first I felt a bit sad. Now only the female snake was left on land. But then I saw clouds of mud in the water and I knew that the other

chessboard a flat piece of wood with sixty-four black and white squares for playing the game of chess

canal a straight river made by people for carrying water to dry land

terrapin a kind of tortoise that lives in warm rivers and lakes

mud very wet ground

slide a thin path that you move down quickly and easily without moving your arms or legs to help you

male an animal that cannot make eggs or have babies

mate (of animals) to make love

snake had gone to rest on the muddy bottom of the canal. I could catch it later.

A water snake

I put my stick on the female snake and pushed her down into the grass. She opened her pink mouth and **hissed** at me. Quickly, I took her round the neck between my finger and thumb, picked her up, and put her into my basket with no problem. Then I went to catch the other snake.

I took off my shoes and got into the canal. I could feel the warm mud between my toes and suddenly I felt the male snake moving under one of my feet. Then he came up to the top of the water and started swimming away. With a shout I threw myself at him and caught him round the neck. When I climbed out of the canal to put the second snake in my basket I saw, to my surprise, that a man was watching me. He was short and thick-bodied, with short hair, blue eyes, a nose like a bird's beak and a wide smiling mouth. I didn't recognize him.

'Your health!' he said in a rich deep voice.

'Thank you, and the same to you!' I replied politely as I put the second snake in with the first, and then washed my hands. After that I took out some grapes from my bag and the stranger and I sat and ate them.

He didn't ask me all the usual questions about my family, so in the end I asked him where he was going. He said he was going down to the beach where he had left his boat. I said I wanted to go to the beach too to get some shellfish to eat. So, we went together.

When we arrived at the beach and found his boat, I asked him where he came from.

'Vido,' he said.

hiss to make a noise like a long 's'; some animals make this noise when they are angry

A black-backed gull

Vido was a small island with a prison on it.

'But Vido's a prison island,' I said.

'That's right,' he answered. 'I'm a prisoner, but I don't make trouble and so they let me sail my boat home for the weekends. I must be back by Monday of course.'

I was not too surprised at this. After all, this was Corfu and anything was possible.

Then I noticed a large black-backed **gull** tied to the man's boat and put my hand out to touch it.

'Careful! He can bite!' said the man, but the gull let me touch it without any problem.

'He likes you,' said the man. 'Do you want him?'

I couldn't believe my ears. 'Thank you,' I said as the man untied the gull and gave him to me.

'I call him Alecko,' said the man. 'He'll come when you call. You'll need some fish for him tomorrow. Come here in the morning and we'll go fishing together.'

Then he got into his boat and got ready to sail away.

'What's your name?' I asked him as he left. 'And why are you in prison?'

'My name's Kosti Panopoulos,' he replied. 'And I killed my wife.'

Slowly his boat sailed away.

'Your health!' called Kosti. 'Until tomorrow!'

When I got home and showed Alecko to everyone they were shocked.

'What's that?' said Mother.

gull a large grey or white bird that lives by the sea

I explained that it was a gull.

'I'm sure they're unlucky,' said Larry.

Then Roger came in to have a closer look at Alecko. The gull almost bit him on the nose and he ran off hurriedly.

'There you are,' said Larry. 'It's been here only five minutes and already it nearly kills the dog.'

'Where did you get him?' asked Leslie.

I explained about my meeting with Kosti and how he had given me the bird. (I didn't say anything about the snakes because Leslie hates snakes.)

'What kind of person is this Kosti?' asked Larry.

'A prisoner,' I said. 'But they let him out at weekends.'

'A prisoner!' cried Mother.

'I'm going fishing with him tomorrow,' I added.

'Is that safe?' asked Mother. 'I mean, you don't know what he's in prison for.'

'Yes, I do. He killed his wife!'

'A murderer!' cried Mother.

In the end Mother said I could go fishing with Kosti if Leslie went with me. When we had enough fish for Alecko for a week, I asked Kosti to come up to the villa to meet Mother.

'He seems a really nice man!' she said after he'd left. 'He doesn't look like a murderer at all.'

I had many more adventures with my family and other animals on Corfu. Kosti finally helped me to catch Old Plop the terrapin. Leslie found my two water snakes hissing at him in the bath one hot day and was so frightened that he nearly killed me. (I had only put them in cold water because they had been out in the sun too long!) Then there was the dinner party when Alecko got under the table and bit everyone's legs.

But all good things must come to an end, and this is what happened to my fun and games on Corfu. Mother had found me one last teacher on the island – Mr Kralefsky. He was a funny-looking little man, with an egg-shaped head and a very rounded back. On my first visit to his home, he didn't teach me anything. Instead, he introduced me to his birds, which he kept in large **cages** at the top of his house. Kralefsky moved about quickly, dancing from one cage to the next giving his birds clean water. As he jumped around he didn't stop talking, though I was never sure if he was speaking to me or the birds. Although I enjoyed helping Mr Kralefsky to look after his birds, his lessons were very boring. He just wanted me to learn things by heart all the time. Finally, after some months, he told Mother that he had taught me everything and that I needed to finish my schooling somewhere like England or Switzerland.

I was against the idea, but Mother had decided that we should go back to England. When she realized that the rest of the family were also against moving away, she told us that it would only be for a short holiday and that we could come back to Corfu later.

So we packed our boxes, bags and suitcases, and put tortoises and birds in baskets and cages. We took our last sad walks through the olive trees and said goodbye to all our village friends. On the day we left, Spiro, Theodore and Mr Kralefsky came to say goodbye to us.

'Well . . . er . . . see you soon,' said Theodore.

'Goodbye! Goodbye!' said Kralefsky to each of us. 'And, I say, you must make the most of your stay in old England. Make it a real holiday, eh.'

Spiro shook each of our hands and then began to cry.

'I'm sorry,' he said, his large stomach shaking. 'I don't mean to cry, but it's just like saying goodbye to my own people. I feel like you belong to me.'

Then we got on the ship. As it moved away across the sea we looked back and saw our three friends at the water's edge. Theodore, standing straight and serious, was waving goodbye with his stick, Kralefsky was jumping up and down crazily, and Spiro was crying one minute and waving sadly at us with one of his fat hands the next.

cage a wooden box made of wooden or metal sticks to keep an animal in

As we left Corfu behind, a black sadness filled our hearts and lasted all the way to England. We got the train from Brindisi towards Switzerland and sat in silence, not wanting to talk. Roger slept at our feet. The birds sang in their cages, and Alecko gave a sad cry from time to time.

circus a travelling show, with clowns, animals and music

When we got to Switzerland an unsmiling policeman climbed onto the train to check our passports. When he had finished looking at the passports, he wrote something on a piece of paper. Then he gave everything back to Mother and got off the train.

Mother read the paper with a shocked look on her face.

'What an awful man. Just look what he's written!' she said angrily, showing the paper to us.

We looked at the words, which said in black ink: *ONE TRAVELLING **CIRCUS**, GOING TO ENGLAND.*

'What a strange thing to write,' said Mother. 'I can't think why he put that!'

The chessboard fields

READING CHECK

Are these sentences true or false? Tick the boxes.   **True** **False**

a Gerry catches two fat brown water beetles.   ☐   ☑

b Gerry meets a man called Kosti who comes from a nearby prison island. ☐ ☐

c Kosti was sent to prison because he murdered his wife.   ☐   ☐

d Kosti takes Gerry round the island on his boat.   ☐   ☐

e Kosti gives Gerry a large gull as a present.   ☐   ☐

f Mr Kralefsky, a bird lover, becomes Gerry's next teacher. ☐   ☐

g After some months Mr Kralefsky says Gerry must go to school in town. ☐ ☐

h Mother decides to take her family back to England.   ☐   ☐

i Kralefsky, Theodore and Spiro come to the airport to say goodbye to the Durrells. ☐ ☐

j Happiness fills the Durrells' hearts when they leave Corfu. ☐   ☐

k The Swiss policeman who gets on their train thinks the Durrell family is strange. ☐ ☐

WORD WORK

1 Match the words with the correct pictures.

a ~~cheessboard~~
......gull.........

b cages
....

c terrapin
....

d circus
....

e canal
....

f gull
....

2 Correct the boxed words in these sentences.

a The female snake **kisses** when Gerry catches it. ......*hisses*......

b Gerry gets into the canal to catch the **pale** snake. ....

c The second snake escapes down a **glide** . ...

d It hides in **bud** under the water. ....

e Many animals **date** in spring. ....

GUESS WHAT

What happens after the story ends? Tick the boxes.

a ☐ The Durrell family spend three months in England and then return to Corfu.

b ☐ Margo meets Peter again in England and marries him.

c ☐ Margo goes back to Corfu and marries Theodore.

d ☐ Spiro travels to England and marries Mother.

e ☐ Leslie becomes a famous sports star.

f ☐ Larry becomes a famous writer.

g ☐ Gerry becomes a famous writer.

h ☐ Gerry spends his life working with animals.

PROJECT A *A letter to a friend*

1 Read this letter and answer the questions.

  a Who is the letter from?

  b Which chapter in the book is it about?

> *Dearest Sophie,*
>
> *I'm writing to tell you about this wonderful boy that I met two weeks ago. He's tall and really handsome with dark wavy hair. I met him at the beach; he's a really good swimmer. He came for tea yesterday. He kissed Mother's hand and smiled at everybody. Mother talked to him nicely but the rest of the family just looked at him and didn't say anything. They weren't very polite, I must say.*
>
> *He tried to talk to my brother Larry about writing but Larry wasn't interested and looked down his nose at him. Then he talked about swimming and riding horses and sailing boats while he drank his tea. I think he's lovely. Tomorrow we're going to the cinema. Mother is going to come with us.*
>
> *I'll write and tell you more later.*
>
> *Love,*

2 Complete the table on page 73 with information from the letter.

Opening of letter:	Dearest Sophie
Who is she writing about?	
What does he look like?	
Where did she meet him?	
What is he like?	
What happened?	
What are her feelings towards him?	
What's going to happen?	
Closing of letter:	

3 **Look at Chapter 8 and write a letter from Peter about meeting someone new. Use the information in the table.**

Opening of letter:	*Dear Jack*
Who is he writing about?	*Margo*
What does she look like?	*very beautiful face and lovely eyes*
Where did he meet her?	*at the villa where I go to give lessons to Gerry Durrell*
What is she like?	*very friendly and loves talking*
What happened?	*she showed me lots of different plants and held my hand and kissed me; went rowing and swimming in the sea by moonlight*
What's going to happen?	*we're going to leave Corfu together and get married in England*
Closing of letter:	*Your friend,*

4 **In the story *My Family and Other Animals* Gerald Durrell meets lots of interesting people. Write a letter from Gerry to one of his friends, describing the time when he meets one of the people below.**

Kosti   Kralefsky   Spiro   Theodore   the Rose-beetle Man   Yani

PROJECT B *Animal facts*

1 **Read this fact sheet about cicadas and answer the questions.**

Cicadas

When baby cicadas come out of their eggs they are wingless. They dig down and live under the ground for a number of years. When a young cicada becomes an adult it climbs up above ground. It pushes out of its old skin and comes out with wings.

An adult cicada has a thick body with two pairs of wings and three pairs of legs. It has two large eyes on each side of its head, and three small eyes on the top of its head. Both young and adult cicadas drink the sugary water from the inside of plants. Cicadas can see and hear very well. They hide from birds that want to eat them, or fly away. They are awake in the day. Only the male cicadas make a noise; they sing on sunny days while resting on trees. In the past, cicadas were eaten in Australia, China, Greece, South America, and Africa. Chinese doctors use them as medicine for earache.

a Do cicadas come from eggs or are they born?

b Where do they live when they're young? For how long?

c How many legs and wings do they have?

d How many eyes do they have and where are they?

e What food do they live on?

f How do they escape attack from other animals?

g When are they awake?

h Are there differences between males and females?

i What other interesting facts about them do you know?

2 Read these notes about scorpions and complete the fact sheet below.

Babies	*are born white and soft*
	stay on their mother's back for one or two weeks
Adults	*2 large claws*
	4 pairs of legs
	tail filled with poison
	2 eyes in the middle of their body (and smaller eyes on each side)
Food	*insects, spiders, baby scorpions*
	don't like beetles
	larger scorpions eat snakes
	wait for food to come near

How they escape	*can't see very well*
	can feel things and smell
Awake	*at night*
Other facts	*female usually eats male after mating*
	shine pale green in dark

Scorpions

When baby scorpions .... they are .... They climb up onto their .... for .... When young scorpions are ready they push out of their old skin and start to look like real scorpions. An adult scorpion has a long body with .... at the front and four .... At the back it has a .... with .... Scorpions have .... in the middle of their bodies and .... on each side. Adult scorpions eat .... They don't like eating .... Larger scorpions .... They usually catch food by .... Scorpions .... very well, but they .... moving under their feet and can .... things too. They are awake .... Scorpions dance together and kiss before they mate. The ....…... the male afterwards. Scorpions .... in the dark.

3 Read the notes and write a fact sheet about praying mantises or geckos.

	Praying Mantises	**Geckos**
Babies	are born from eggs	are born from eggs
	very small and wingless	very small and you can see through them
	live on plants for a number of months (walk one behind the other)	mother comes to give food
	grow a new skin 12 times before they become an adult	young geckos grow a new skin many times as they get older
Adults	long body	long pale green body
	1 pair large claws at front	4 legs
	2 pairs legs	tail
	wings at back	2 large eyes at the top of its head (geckos can't close their eyes and they clean them with their tongue)
	2 large eyes on the side of its head	
Food	often young mantises eat brother or sister as first meal and after that small flies	spiders, flies, other insects
	adults eat butterflies, beetles, spiders, geckos, small birds	
How they escape	can see very well 	tail falls off when a larger animal attacks
		can see very well
		can climb up walls, across ceilings, and even up glass – they have small hairs on their feet to help them
Awake	some mantises in the day and some at night	at night
Other facts	male jumps on female's back before they mate	the female is smaller than the male
	female often eats male after mating, starting with his head	get their name from the call they make, 'gecko! gecko!'
	can turn their heads right round to look backwards	

GRAMMAR CHECK

Past Simple and Past Perfect

We use the Past Simple to talk about things that happened at a specific time in the past and that are now finished.

Gerald and his family left England and went to live in Corfu.

We use the Past Perfect for actions that happened before other things in the past.

Larry's friend George had gone to live in Corfu before the Durrell family arrived.

1 Complete the sentences. Use the Past Simple or Past Perfect form of the verbs in brackets.

a When he saw that his family ..had become.. (become) ill, Larry wanted to go abroad.

b The family packed their bags and .... (travel) to Corfu through France, Switzerland, and Italy.

c Spiro .... (spend) several years in Chicago before he returned to Corfu.

d The Rose-beetle man .... (not speak), but .... he (move) his hands and face a lot.

2 Complete the text. Use the Past Simple or Past Perfect form of the words in the box.

~~live~~	have	bring	be	arrive	learn
die	move	make	write	stay	

Gerald tells the story of his family who a) ..lived.. in Corfu in the 1930s. His father b) .... some years before. When they c) .... on the island, they d) .... boxes full of books and clothes that they e) .... with them from England.

At first the family f) .... in a hotel. Later they g) .... into a villa outside the town. After a few months, they h) .... friends with lots of people. After several years on the island, Gerald i) .... all about the animals in his new home. In later life he j) .... about his time on Corfu and how important it k) .... to him.

GRAMMAR CHECK

Relative clauses with who, what, where, and when

We use **who** to introduce relative clauses about people.

Theo was the man who gave Gerald a pocket microscope.

We use **what** to introduce relative clauses about things.

A tortoise was what Gerald bought from the Rose-beetle man.

We use **where** to introduce relative clauses about places.

Corfu was the island where Gerald and his family went to live.

We use **when** to introduce relative clauses about times.

Gerald spoke Greek well when he finally left Corfu.

We do not use commas with this kind of relative clause because the sentence is not complete without it.

3 **Complete these sentences with *who, what, where,* or *when*.**

  a Studying animals is ...*what*.. Gerald loves.

  b Writing is .... Larry does every day.

  c The strawberry-pink villa is .... the Durrells first lived.

  d Spiro is the man .... finds the villa for the family.

  e George's house is .... Gerald meets Theo.

  f Springtime is .... Margo meets a young man on the beach.

  g The cinema is .... Margo's new boyfriend takes her.

  h Cooking is .... Mrs Durrell enjoys doing for her family.

  i Yani is the man .... takes care of the goats.

  j A scorpion is .... Gerald puts in a matchbox.

  k Thursdays are .... Gerald and Theo go for long walks.

  l Aunt Hermione is the woman .... writes to Gerald's mother.

  m Vido is the island .... Kosti is a prisoner.

  n The beach is .... Gerald and Kosti go together.

  o On the train, they meet a Swiss policeman .... thinks that they are a travelling circus.

  p Travelling from Corfu to England is .... the Durrells felt very sad.

GRAMMAR

GRAMMAR CHECK

Gerund with sense verbs

The gerund (–ing form) is the noun form of a verb. To make the gerund, we usually add –ing to the verb, but when a verb ends in a consonant + –e, we remove the e and add –ing.

sing – singing   move – moving

When a verb ends in a consonant + vowel + consonant, we double the final consonant and add –ing.

swim – swimming   run – running

We use the gerund after sense verbs such as hear, see, feel, smell, watch, listen to and notice.

They heard the cicadas singing above the noise of the ship's engine.

4 Complete the sentences. Use the *–ing* form of the verbs in brackets.

a Gerald felt the flat rocks ..warming. (warm) his back.

b He listened to the rest of his family .... (talk) for hours.

c He went swimming and felt something .... (move) around in the dark waters near him.

d He saw a porpoise .... (swim) quickly past him.

e He watched the porpoises .... (jump) playfully in and out of the sea.

f Gerald watched Theo .... (walk) up to the house.

g Theo heard the plane .... (come) nearer and nearer.

h Theo and Gerald listened to the insects .... (sing) in the grass.

i Theo watched the sea-plane .... (land) on the water.

j Gerald listened to Theo .... (tell) a funny story about his friend.

k Theo and Gerald watched Roger .... (run) happily in front of them.

l Theo watched Gerald and his family .... (leave) the island.

m Theo saw the boat .... (disappear) little by little.

IIIIIIIII

GRAMMAR CHECK

Modal auxiliary verbs: ought to and should

We use ought to + infinitive or should + infinitive without *to* to give advice about what is the right thing to do.

We ought to go and live somewhere warm and sunny.

We should leave England!

We use shouldn't + infinitive without *to* to form negative statements.

Margo shouldn't spend so much time alone with that young man. (= it's a bad thing)

We normally use should + subject + infinitive without *to* for questions.

What should we take to Corfu? Books? Clothes? Medicine?

5 **Spiro is giving advice to the Durrells. Complete the sentences with the phrases in the box.**

shouldn't show	should stay	shouldn't listen	ought to have
~~should listen~~	shouldn't worry	~~ought to go~~	
shouldn't go	should get	should move	

a 'You .*should listen*. to me if you want to learn about the island.'

b 'You .*ought to go*. and live in that pink villa on the hill.'

c 'You .... into my car. Don't use these others!'

d 'You .... your mother, Gerald.'

e 'You .... to all those other drivers. They know nothing!'

f 'Miss Margo .... swimming with that young man. It's dangerous!'

g 'Gerald .... lessons with Theodore. He's a good teacher.'

h 'You .... to the yellow villa because it's bigger, and you need a bigger house now.'

i 'You .... those toads to me, Gerald. They make me feel sick!'

j 'You .... in Corfu. It's beautiful here!'

GRAMMAR

GRAMMAR CHECK

Used to

Used to refers to past habits and states. These are things that we did or felt repeatedly in the past, but we do not do them or feel them now. To make the affirmative form, we use used + to + infinitive.

Before they went to Corfu, Gerald's family used to live in England.

To make the negative and question forms, we use didn't/did + use + to + infinitive.

They didn't use to be in very good health.

Did they use to go swimming?

6 Read Gerald's notebook. Then complete the text with *used to* and the verbs in the box.

not spend	be	have	not go	~~live~~
catch	enjoy	not run	ache	go

Corfu, 1936

When I was in England, I a) ...used to live... in Bournemouth. The weather often b) .... cold and wet there. Our house was near the beach, but I c) .... swimming very often because it was too cold. My family was often ill. My mother's fingers d) .... and my sister e) .... red spots all over her face.

I've always loved animals and I f) .... butterflies and keep caterpillars in jars. But I g) .... all day outside, as I do now in Corfu. My dog, Roger, has a wonderful time now too. Of course, he always liked going for walks but he h) .... around outside for hours as he does here.

In England, I i) .... to school every day. Here on the island, I have a teacher, Theo, who gives me lessons at home. I'm learning a lot now. I j) .... my lessons much less before!

GRAMMAR CHECK

> **Linkers: so, because, in order to, and although**
>
> We use **so** to link two parts of a sentence talking about the result of something.
>
> *The weather in England was cold so the Durrells went to Corfu.*
>
> We use **because** to link two parts of a sentence talking about the reason for something.
>
> *Mrs Durrell wanted a house outside the town because it would be healthier.*
>
> We use **in order to** to link two parts of a sentence talking about the purpose of something.
>
> *Theo went upstairs in order to watch the sea-plane landing.*
>
> We use **although** to link two parts of a sentence with different ideas.
>
> *Although Mrs Durrell didn't want to move, she finally agreed to buy the yellow villa.*

7 **Complete the sentences with *so, because, in order to*, or *although*.**

a Spiro could speak English ....*so*.... the family decided to go in his taxi.

b .... Mrs Durrell was tired and untidy, she spoke calmly to the hotel manager.

c Mrs Durrell didn't like most of the villas .... they didn't have a bathroom.

d Gerald wanted to visit the island .... he always ate his breakfast as quickly as possible.

e Larry found it difficult to write .... there was a donkey outside his bedroom window.

f Gerald tied his tortoise to a tree .... stop him walking off.

g Gerald usually arrived late for his lessons .... he was always on time for natural history.

h Theo wanted to see the trapdoor spiders .... he went with Gerald to look at them.

i Gerald often put insects into jars .... watch them moving their legs.

GRAMMAR

GRAMMAR CHECK

Reported speech and reported questions

In direct speech, we give the words that people say.	In reported speech, we put the verb one step into the past and change the pronouns and possessive adjectives.
'My taxi is the best,' he said.	*He said (that) his taxi was the best.*
'The birds have gone!' she said.	*She said (that) the birds had gone.*

We can use *that* to introduce a reported statement, but it is not necessary.

We report questions using reported speech affirmative sentence construction, but we do not use *that*. In *Wh–* questions, the question word – *when, who, where, why* – introduces the reported question.

'What languages do you speak?' I asked her.   *I asked her what languages she spoke.*

8 Rewrite the direct speech as reported speech.

a 'Why do we stay in this country?' asked Larry.

Larry asked why they stayed in that country.

b 'I've had a letter from George this morning,' said Larry.

....

c 'We can't sell our house,' Mrs Durrell said to her children.

....

d 'I'll take Roger with me,' said Gerald.

....

e 'What are we waiting for?' Larry asked his family.

....

....

f 'We'll soon be at the hotel,' said Mrs Durrell.

....

....

g 'Where are our rooms?' she asked the hotel manager.

....

....

Dominoes is an enjoyable series of illustrated classic and modern stories in four carefully graded language stages – from Starter to Three – which take learners from beginner to intermediate level.

Each *Domino* reader includes:
- **a good story** to read and enjoy
- **integrated activities** to develop reading skills and increase active vocabulary
- **personalized projects** to make the language and story themes more meaningful
- **seven pages of grammar activities** for consolidation.

Each *Domino* pack contains a reader, plus a MultiROM with:
- **a complete audio recording of the story,** fully dramatized to bring it to life
- **interactive activities** to offer further practice in reading and language skills and to consolidate learning.

If you liked this Level Three *Domino*, why not read these?

Dian and the Gorillas
Norma Shapiro

Over the years hunters, poachers, and war have killed many of the gorillas of central Africa. But there are still a few hundred living high in the mists of the Virunga Mountains.

When Dian Fossey first saw a family of wild mountain gorillas in the Virungas she knew that she must help these wonderful animals. This true story tells of the twenty years she lived with them, watched them, wrote about them, and protected them. In the end, she gave her life for them.

Book ISBN: 978 0 19 424827 3
MultiROM Pack ISBN: 978 0 19 424785 6

Mansfield Park
Jane Austen

'Why shouldn't we offer to take care of her? She could live with us at Mansfield.'

In this way Mrs Norris persuades her sister, Lady Bertram, and Lady Bertram's husband, Sir Thomas, to ask their poor niece Fanny Price to live with them at Mansfield Park.

At first Fanny is unhappy there. Then, after she makes friends with her young cousins, things improve. But what happens when the cousins are older, and starting to think of love?

Book ISBN: 978 0 19 424828 0
MultiROM Pack ISBN: 978 0 19 424786 3

You can find details and a full list of books in the *Dominoes* catalogue and Oxford English Language Teaching Catalogue, and on the website: www.oup.com/elt

Teachers: see www.oup.com/elt for a full range of online support, or consult your local office.

	CEF	Cambridge Exams	IELTS	TOEFL iBT	TOEIC
Starter	A1	YLE Movers	–	–	–
Level 1	A1–A2	YLE Flyers/KET	3.0	–	–
Level 2	A2–B1	KET-PET	3.0-4.0	–	–
Level 3	B1	PET	4.0	57-86	550